James Joyce Revisited

Twayne's English Authors Series

Kinley E. Roby, Editor

Northeastern University

TEAS 490

JAMES JOYCE (1882–1941)
Printed with the permission of Morris Library, Southern Illinois University at Carbondale

James Joyce Revisited

Richard F. Peterson

Southern Illinois University

Twayne Publishers • New York
Maxwell Macmillan Canada • Toronto
Maxwell Macmillan International • New York Oxford Singapore Sydney

James Joyce Revisited
Richard F. Peterson

Twayne Publishers   Maxwell Macmillan Canada, Inc.
Macmillan Publishing Company   1200 Eglinton Avenue East
866 Third Avenue   Suite 200
New York, New York 10022   Don Mills, Ontario M3C 3N1

Macmillan Publishing Company is part of the Maxwell Communication Group of
Companies.

Library of Congress Cataloging-in-Publication Data

Peterson, Richard F.
    James Joyce revisited / Richard F. Peterson.
        p.   cm.—(Twayne's English authors series; TEAS 490)
    Includes bibliographical references (p. 123) and index.
    ISBN 0-8057-7016-X: $24.95
    1. Joyce, James, 1882-1941—Criticism and interpretation.
I. Title. II. Series.
PR6019.09Z7816   1992
823'.912—dc20   91-33735
                                                CIP

The paper used in this publication meets the minimum requirements
of American National Standard for Information Sciences—Permanence
of Paper for Printed Library Materials. ANSI Z3948-1984. ⊗™

10 9 8 7 6 5 4

Printed in the United States of America

For my mother, Lillian Peterson

Contents

Preface

The title *James Joyce Revisited* seems appropriate for Twayne's English Author Series and for an introduction to Joyce's life and works. With this volume the series revisits James Joyce 25 years after publishing A. Walton Litz's excellent introduction. While acknowledging the earlier volume, the title also recognizes that any new introduction to Joyce is a revisiting, not only within the Twayne series but within the larger context of Joyce criticism. Measuring Joyce's towering presence in modern literature, burrowing through the intricacies of his language and style, and discovering his vision and form of forms have become an irresistible, seemingly inexhaustible "funferal" in Joyce studies.

For my own introduction to Joyce I decided to revisit the classroom in search of those aspects of Joyce's work which make him most accessible and inviting to students. From the perspective of teaching Joyce I have discovered that Joyce's own teachings—his comments and commentaries on the art of his fiction—often provide the most immediate access to his literature. That Joyce has marked out his own best introduction to the labyrinth of his art is hardly surprising, considering he often wrote about his work either to justify its existence or to convince reluctant readers that his writing was well worth their effort.

James Joyce Revisited, after an opening chapter that traces Joyce's life through the private and public ordeals of his artistic mission, follows his career from the early lyrical impulses to the unrelenting scrupulous meanness of his reflections on Dublin life and his developing portrait of the artist arrested at the critical stage of young manhood. The later chapters then track Joyce through his greatest achievements: his odyssey through the consciousness of modern life and his inquiry into the night world of human existence. The final chapter concludes the revisit by examining Joyce's contemporaneity within the context of both literary tradition and innovation and critical and theoretical study.

Several years ago I had the opportunity to prepare a volume on William Butler Yeats for this series. In my preface to that book— which coincidentally was published the year of the Joyce centennial—I wrote that, while in graduate school, I was asked by a distinguished Joyce scholar to name the eponymous figure of the age and, avoiding the obvious answer, had selected William Butler Yeats. I do not know if I am any wiser than I was in graduate school or when I wrote the Yeats book, but I am aware, after writing the present volume on Joyce, of the cyclical nature of even the critical and academic world and the irresistible attraction of the coincidence of contraries.

Acknowledgments

"Excerpts" from *Dubliners,* by James Joyce. Copyright 1916 by B. W. Huebsch. Definitive text Copyright © 1967 by the estate of James Joyce. Used by permission of Viking Penguin, a division of Penguin Books USA Inc. and Jonathan Cape Ltd. as executors of the James Joyce Estate.

From *A Portrait of the Artist as a Young Man,* by James Joyce. Copyright 1916 by B. W. Huebsch, copyright 1944 by Nora Joyce, copyright © 1964 by the Estate of James Joyce. Used by permission of Viking Penguin, a division of Penguin Books USA Inc., and Jonathan Cape Ltd. as executors of the James Joyce Estate.

From *Ulysses, The Corrected Text,* by James Joyce. Reading text copyright © 1984 by the Trustees of the Estate of James Joyce. Preface copyright © 1986 by Richard Ellmann. Afterword copyright © 1986 by Hans Walter Gabler. Reprinted by permission of Random House, Inc.

From *Finnegans Wake,* by James Joyce. Copyright 1939 by James Joyce. Copyright renewed © by George Joyce and Lucia Joyce. Used by permission of Viking Penguin, Inc., a division of Penguin Books USA Inc., and the Society of Authors as literary representatives of the James Joyce Estate.

Though I am grateful for the help of many Joyce scholars, I wish to make special acknowledgment of the generous support, encouragement, and friendship of Margaret Church, Edmund Epstein, Alan Cohn, and Bernard Benstock. I have had the good fortune of beginning my career with Edmund Epstein as my senior colleague, of receiving many kindnesses from Margaret Church in my early scholarly travels, of learning from and eventually collaborating with Alan Cohn, and of benefiting, since my days in graduate school, from the counsel of Bernard Benstock, who graciously recommended to Twayne that I write this book. Finally, I wish to express my deep appreciation to Pauline Duke, for her dedicated work in preparing the manuscript.

Chronology

1882   James Joyce born 2 February at 41 Brighton Square West in Rathgar, a south Dublin suburb.

1888   Sent to Clongowes Wood College, a prestigious Jesuit school 40 miles from Dublin.

1893   Enters Belvedere College, a Jesuit day school, as the family, after several changes in residences necessitated by declining finances, moves from the Dublin suburbs to the city itself.

1898   Enrolls at University College as family continues a series of moves about Dublin.

1900   Reads a paper, "Drama and Life," to the Literary and Historical Society and publishes a review of Ibsen's *When We Dead Awaken.* Also writes a play, *A Brilliant Career,* which he later destroys.

1901   Has privately printed "The Day of the Rabblement," his essay attacking the Irish Literary Theatre, after the essay is rejected by *St. Stephen's,* a student magazine.

1902   His paper on the Irish poet James Clarence Mangan is delivered to the literary society and published in *St. Stephen's.* After graduating from the university, travels to Paris to study medicine.

1903   Returns to Ireland in April because of his mother's serious illness; her death, in August, will become central to the narrative of *Ulysses.*

1904   Writes three stories for the *Irish Homestead* and an essay, "A Portrait of the Artist." With Nora Barnacle, leaves Dublin for the Continent in October. Though the expected teaching position in Zurich is not available, he finds a position in Pola.

1905   With Nora, moves to Trieste and takes a teaching position at the Berlitz School; Georgio, the couple's first child, born in July. Joyce's brother Stanislaus arrives in October. Joyce sends *Chamber Music* and an early version of *Dubliners* to a Dublin publisher.

1906   Takes a position in a Rome bank. Adds two stories to *Dubliners,* which Grant Richards accepts for publication.

1907   Returns to Trieste with Nora; daughter, Lucia, born in July. *Chamber Music* published by Elkin Mathews as Joyce adds "The Dead" to *Dubliners* and begins revising *Stephen Hero*, the autobiographical novel that has evolved from the essay "A Portrait of the Artist."

1909   Makes two trips to Ireland. Arranges for Maunsel and Company to publish *Dubliners* and, representing a Triestine group of investors, sets up the first movie theater in Dublin; the theater fails the following year, as does the agreement to publish *Dubliners*.

1912   Makes his last visit to Ireland. On failing to rescue *Dubliners* for publication, writes the broadside "Gas from a Burner."

1914   His annus mirabilis: Grant Richards, several years after the initial contract, publishes *Dubliners;* serialization of *A Portrait of the Artist as a Young Man* begins in the *Egoist;* and he starts *Exiles* and *Ulysses.*

1915   Joyce family forced by World War I to move to Zurich.

1916   *A Portrait of the Artist as a Young Man* published.

1917   Undergoes the first of many eye operations; also, however, completes the first three chapters of *Ulysses.*

1918   The *Little Review* begins serialization of *Ulysses. Exiles* published in London.

1919   With the war over, the Joyce family returns to Trieste.

1920   At the urging of Ezra Pound, Joyce takes his family to Paris in July. The serialization of *Ulysses* is stopped by court order and subsequent trial.

1922   *Ulysses* published by Sylvia Beach through her Shakespeare and Company bookstore in Paris; Joyce receives an advance copy on his birthday.

1923   Begins writing *Finnegans Wake.*

1924   First Fragment of *Finnegans Wake* published under "Work in Progress" in *transatlantic review.*

1927   *Pomes Penyeach,* a collection of poems, published by Shakespeare and Company. Additional fragments of *Work in Progress,* the title he temporarily adopts for *Finnegans Wake,* published.

1931   He and Nora are married in July at a registry office in London. His father dies in December.

1932 Grandson, Stephen, born in February. Lucia Joyce suffers her first mental breakdown.

1933 In a celebrated court decision, Judge Woolsey rules that *Ulysses* is not pornography and may be published and sold in the United States.

1934 Random House, under the editorship of Bennett Cerf, publishes an American edition of *Ulysses*.

1936 *Collected Poems* published.

1939 *Finnegans Wake* published on 4 May, though Joyce receives an advance copy for his birthday. When World War II begins, the Joyces leave Paris to be near Lucia, who is hospitalized in Vichy.

1940 The Joyces manage to leave occupied France for Zurich, but Lucia remains in Vichy at a mental hospital. Herbert Gorman's biography, closely supervised by Joyce, is published.

1941 Joyce dies, after complications from surgery for a perforated ulcer, on 13 January, less than a month before his fifty-ninth birthday.

Chapter One
Welcome, O Life: The Odyssey of Joyce

Once upon a time—2 February 1882, to be precise—James Joyce was born to John and May Joyce at 41 Brighton Square West in Rathgar, a south Dublin suburb.[1] Joyce's birth came, however, at what was not necessarily a very good time for the Joyce family and what was hardly a very good time in Irish history. The secondborn but the first of 10 surviving children, James Augusta Joyce entered the domestic life of the Joyce family just after his father had taken out the first mortgage on one of his Cork properties and moved from Kingstown to Rathgar.[2] Born a Roman Catholic and British subject, Joyce also arrived just after the Irish leader Charles Stewart Parnell had been arrested by English authorities for coercion and imprisoned in Kilmainham Jail.

While the Joyce family was in no immediate danger of financial collapse in early 1882, James Joyce was to live his youth entangled in his father's financial and domestic misadventures. The economic decline of the Joyce family appears impressionistically in the autobiographical *A Portrait of the Artist as a Young Man* as early as the second chapter, where Stephen Dedalus sits with his "redeyed mother" during one of the family's frequent moves and later listens to his father railing against his "enemies."[3] By the last chapter Stephen, confronted and offended by the economic collapse of his family, rejects all claims of authority, including that of his father, described as, among many things, "a bankrupt and at present a praiser of his own past" (*P*, 241).

Joyce was also to live his youth during a political decade in Irish history charged by the personality and career of Charles Stewart Parnell. While Parnell was released from Kilmainham three months after Joyce's birth and was to emerge with even greater power and influence, his career remained controversial until he was driven out of politics in 1890 by the scandal surrounding his relationship with a married woman, Katharine O'Shea. Parnell's fall and subsequent death in 1891 so angered young Joyce that he wrote a poem, "Et Tu, Healy," denouncing Tim Healy, Parnell's close political aide, for betraying the Irish leader.[4] Throughout his life and career, Joyce closely identified with Parnell, whose ghostly presence haunts the first chapter of *A Portrait* and the Hades episode of *Ulysses*. In an article for *Il piccolo della sera*, Joyce described Parnell as a hunted deer, brought down by his own people: "In his final desperate appeal to his countrymen, he begged them not to throw him as a sop to the English wolves howling around them. It redounds to their honour that they did not fail this appeal. They did not throw him to the English wolves; they tore him to pieces themselves."[5]

Portrait of a Young Man

In his biography Richard Ellmann describes Joyce in his youth as "a well-behaved, slim little boy" of such "serene disposition" that his family called him "Sunny Jim" (Ellmann, 26). In September 1888 Joyce's father, filled with great ambition for his oldest son, sent him to Clongowes Wood College, a prestigious Jesuit school 40 miles from Dublin. At Clongowes from 1888 to 1891, Joyce moved to the head of his class in his studies, while further developing a keen interest in church ritual that would remain with him even after he had rejected the Catholic religion, and would deeply influence his writing.

Joyce's education at Clongowes ended in 1891 when John Joyce, plagued by increasing debts, withdrew his son from the Jesuit school. By 1893 the children were sent to the Christian Brothers' school, taught by a brotherhood of Catholic laity, as the family for the first time was forced to move into the city of Dublin. Fortunately for young Joyce, his father was able to make arrangements for each of his sons to attend Belvedere College, a Jesuit day school. There the oldest son continued to excel in his studies, especially English composition; indeed, at age 15 Joyce received a £3 prize for the best composition written by a student at his grade level.

In *A Portrait of the Artist* Stephen Dedalus envisions university life as "a new adventure" as well as an escape from "the sentries who had stood as guardians of his boyhood and had sought to keep him among them that he might be subject to them and serve their ends" (*P*, 165). For Joyce, his enrollment in September 1898 at University College, Dublin, marked the beginning of several key friendships, including one with John Byrne, the Cranly of *A Portrait*, and gave him the opportunity to expand his study of language and literature. Joyce's enthusiasm for the academic life and his class standing had, however, already faded in his last year at Belvedere, as he became more and more the iconoclast in his attitudes toward religion, nationalism, and family.

The new adventure anticipated by Stephen Dedalus did not begin for Joyce until his second year at University College, when he read a paper on "Drama and Life" to the Literary and Historical Society. Provoked by the society's initial reluctance to accept his paper, Joyce also offered to write an article on the plays of Henrik Ibsen for the *Fortnightly Review* and in return received an invitation to review *When We Dead Awaken.* The controversy generated by Joyce's paper—which, in the fashion of Ibsen, defended drama as the enemy of convention and the champion of truth—and the stunning appearance of his review gave Joyce both notoriety and credibility. When he received a message from English dramatist and critic William Archer that Ibsen himself had written a note of appreciation for Joyce's review, Joyce believed that finally he was beginning his new adventure as a literary artist.

After a brief London visit with Archer, Joyce's next step, especially after proclaiming drama the purest art form, one in which "the artist forgoes his very self and stands a mediator in awful truth before the veiled face of God" (*CW,* 42), was to write his own play. *A Brilliant Career,* dedicated to the artist's own soul, was in Joyce's words the first true work of his life. The play reflected an adolescent mind infatuated with Ibsen's spirit and was eventually destroyed by Joyce.

While Joyce also wrote a considerable amount of poetry, including a verse drama, during this period, his most important writings were his prose sketches. In *Ulysses* a disillusioned Stephen Dedalus, while wandering Sandymount strand, recalls with bitter self-mockery his "epiphanies" to be "written on green oval leaves, deeply deep, copies to be sent if you died to all the great libraries of the world, including Alexandria."[6] These prose sketches, or epiphanies, defined in *Stephen Hero* as the recording of "a sudden spiritual manifestation"[7] of a moment or event, were, however, critical in turning Joyce's attention to the possibility of writing fiction and were the heralds of *Dubliners.*

Now determined to have a brilliant career as a literary artist, Joyce continued to defy convention and amaze his fellow students. At the beginning of his final year at University College he wrote an essay, "The Day of the Rabblement," which was printed at his own expense after being rejected by the faculty adviser of *St. Stephen's,* the university's student magazine. The essay attacked the Irish Literary Theatre for surrendering "to the popular will" and proclaimed, in a statement important to Joyce's own future, that "until he has freed himself from the mean influences about him—sodden enthusiasm and clever insinuation and every flattering influence of vanity and low ambition—no man is an artist at all" (*CW*, 70–72). In February 1902 Joyce gave to the Literary and Historical Society a less controversial paper on the Irish poet James Clarence Mangan in which he expanded his vision of lofty and lonely genius to include "the holy spirit of joy" (*CW*, 83) as a counterpoint to the inevitable disappointment and bitterness of the poet's life. His paper was so well received that it was published in *St. Stephen's* in May 1902, just a month before he completed his studies at University College.

After leaving the university Joyce went about the apparently sensible business of forming connections with the same literary establishment he had attacked in his paper on the Irish rabblement. Less apparent were his reasons for registering at the Royal University Medical School, though this latter decision became the initial step leading to the first of his five flights into exile. When he encountered the obvious difficulties with his expenses and his studies, Joyce decided with more arrogance than common sense that he would attend medical school in Paris. On 1 December 1902 Joyce, armed with advice and letters of support from William Butler Yeats, Lady Gregory, and others, left Ireland for a destination that at this stage in his career suited his vision and two decades later would satisfy his ambition.

Portrait of the Artist

Joyce's first flight to the Continent lasted only until he came home for the Christmas holiday. Even though he had already given up attending medical school, he returned in January to Paris, where he spent his time composing more poetry and epiphanies, writing several reviews, and jotting down his thoughts, as well as borrowings from Aristotle, on aesthetic theory. While making new friends, including John Millington Synge, Joyce plagued his mother with self-pitying letters that spoke of high intent—"I am feeling very intellectual these times"—and pleaded for money—"I had been without food for 42 hours."[8] The pattern ended abruptly, however, when Joyce received a telegram from his father: "Mother dying come home Father" (*Letters*, 2:41).

The events that occurred between Joyce's return to Ireland in April

1903 and his departure for the Continent in October 1904 profoundly influenced his emotional life and his development as an artist. The death of his mother in August 1903 was so disturbing that years later Joyce would make the theme of *amor matris* and the nightmare vision of his dead mother keys to the narrative of *Ulysses*. As Joyce moved from friendship to friendship, from residence to residence, and from occupation to preoccupation, he also encountered other difficulties, including a brief but painful stay at the Martello tower that would inspire the opening scene and sequences in *Ulysses*.

Yet as he appeared to flounder in his personal life, Joyce, in Ellmann's words, "prepared to become great" (Ellmann, 144). While enduring real and imagined slights, he wrote "A Portrait of the Artist," a narrative essay that, though rejected for publication, would evolve into the long autobiographical novel *Stephen Hero* until it was finally refined a decade later into *A Portrait of the Artist as a Young Man*. During this same period Joyce also wrote more poems, several of which were published, and dashed off "The Holy Office," a broadside directed at his literary contemporaries: "And though they spurn me from their door / My soul shall spurn them evermore" (*CW*, 152). The most important literary event for Joyce, however, came through the good offices of George Russell, one of the Dublin luminaries satirized in "The Holy Office." When Russell asked Joyce to contribute a story for the *Irish Homestead*, Joyce, using Stephen Daedulus as his pseudonym, wrote "The Sisters" and two other stories, "Eveline" and "After the Race," for the paper. He also conceived a plan to develop a series of short stories: "I call the series *Dubliners* to betray the soul of that hemiplegia or paralysis which many consider a city" (*Letters*, 1:55).

Just as the literary map of Joyce's career was now beginning to take shape, he encountered the individual who would give emotional direction and assurance to his life and letters.[9] On 16 June 1904, the date later selected for the events of *Ulysses*, Joyce went for a walk with Nora Barnacle, a young woman from Galway. Within a few months Joyce, convinced he had found companion, confessor, and comforter to his soul, decided that Nora should resign her position at the Finn Hotel and leave Dublin with him. In October Joyce and Nora, in anticipation of a teaching position at a Berlitz school in Zurich, boarded a boat and began a journey that would weave its way through several countries and demand the talent and cunning of a modern Ulysses and the fortitude and patience of a Penelope.

Exiles

The odyssey of Joyce and Nora began with brief visits in London and Paris before they arrived in Zurich, only to discover to their shock that no teaching vacancy existed.[10] Encountering a similar situation in Trieste, they settled briefly and uncomfortably in Pola, where Joyce taught English to naval officers and returned to his writing. Forced by Austrian officials to leave Pola, Joyce and Nora returned to Trieste, a city more to their liking, where Nora gave birth to a son, Giorgio, in July.

Now self-imposed exile, struggling artist, reluctant teacher, and proud father, Joyce remained constant in his commitment to his art, completing versions of *Chamber Music* and *Dubliners* while continuing work on his autobiographical novel. As family man, however, he proved his father's son by accumulating debts, frequently changing residences, and drinking heavily. Desperate for help, he convinced his brother Stanislaus to join him in Trieste, but, even with the additional financial and moral support of his brother, Joyce decided to flee with Nora and Giorgio to Rome, where he took a position in August 1906 as a correspondence clerk for a bank.

Arriving in gloomy spirits, Joyce found Rome not much more than an elaborate graveyard. His domestic turbulence increased—Nora was soon pregnant again—and the fate of his writing remained uncertain. Unable to secure a publisher for *Chamber Music,* he had run into further difficulties when Grant Richards, who had agreed to publish *Dubliners,* objected to certain passages in "Two Gallants," a story recently added to the collection, and to Joyce's use of the word *bloody* in "Grace." While Joyce, after protesting angrily, agreed to concessions, Richards finally decided not to publish *Dubliners* at this time. Unhappy with Richards, now doubtful about the merits of *Chamber Music,* even though the English poet and critic Arthur Symons had secured Elkin Mathews as a publisher, and miserable in Rome, Joyce decided, over his brother's objection, to return to Trieste.

Rearrived in Trieste Joyce tutored, lectured, wrote articles on Irish politics, and awaited with some misgiving the publication of *Chamber Music,* which finally appeared in 1907. As expected, his first book brought little literary notice beyond a few favorable reviews and nothing in the way of royalties.[11] While Nora gave birth to a daughter, Lucia, on 26 July 1907, the birth took place in a pauper's ward at the same time that Joyce was hospitalized with rheumatic fever. Supported for the most part by his brother, Joyce managed to rewrite the first

three chapters of *Stephen Hero; Dubliners,* however, was passed unsuccessfully from publisher to publisher as Joyce languished for the next few
years in his personal misfortunes.

With the life of exile going badly, Joyce decided in 1909 to take
Giorgio for a visit to relatives in Dublin and Galway. While in Dublin
he also hoped to secure a publisher for *Dubliners* and a professorship in
Italian at University College. Joyce found a publisher for *Dubliners,* but
Maunsel and Company would prove just as reluctant and troublesome
as Grant Richards. All Joyce really achieved, beyond aggravating Nora
by accusing her of a liaison with another man during their Dublin
courtship, was to bring Eva, one of Joyce's six unmarried sisters, back
with Giorgio and him to Trieste.[12] A month later Joyce again visited
Dublin, this time with a scheme and some financial backing to set up
the city's first cinema, which he actually accomplished when the Volta
opened briefly in December 1909. When he returned to Trieste in early
1910 with yet another sister, Joyce, however, soon learned of the
Volta's financial collapse and of Maunsel's resistance to publishing
Dubliners.

By 1912 Joyce, still struggling with domestic, financial, and publishing woes, decided on still another visit to Ireland, but this one
would be his last. In July Nora and Lucia arrived in Dublin on their
way to Galway, where Joyce and Giorgio joined them a few weeks later.
What began as a hopeful, idyllic journey that included a stay with
Nora's relatives and a trip to the Aran Islands turned nightmarish when
Joyce, returning to Dublin, discovered that Maunsel, fearing libel
because of the anti-Irish nature of the stories, had decided not to
publish *Dubliners,* even though it had been set in type. On 11 September, the proof sheets of *Dubliners* now destroyed, Joyce abandoned all
hope and left Ireland with his family. He did, however, fire one more
broadside at his enemies by writing "Gas from a Burner," in which the
mock-voice of his publisher claims that after 10 years,

> The darkness of my mind was rent
> And I saw the writer's foul intent.
> But I owe a duty to Ireland:
> I hold her honour in my hand,
> This lovely land that always sent
> Her writers and artists to banishment
> And in a spirit of Irish fun
> Betrayed her own leaders, one by one. (*CW*, 243)

Ulysses

If, as Ellmann claims, 1912 was "the most disheartening" year of
Joyce's life, then the next few years, especially the "*annus mirabilis*" of
1914, would prove the most encouraging (Ellmann, 318, 353). This
new direction in Joyce's career began at the end of 1913 when he
received letters from an old adversary seeking to make amends and a
new friend destined to become Joyce's first true apostle. After so many
ordeals Joyce was finally and unexpectedly presented with the actuality
of publishing what for 10 years he had forged in the smithy of his soul.

First Grant Richards, who had reneged on a contract eight years
earlier, expressed a renewed interest in publishing *Dubliners*. Less than a
month later Ezra Pound, prompted by Yeats, offered assistance in
placing Joyce's writing. In early 1914 as Joyce completed negotiations
with Richards, Pound moved quickly to secure Joyce's future in modern literature. By the time *Dubliners* was published in June 1914, *A
Portrait of the Artist as a Young Man* was appearing, through Pound's
arrangement, in serial form in the *Egoist,* which ran the novel from 2
February, Joyce's birthday, to September 1915.[13] With his genius
newly discovered and the path to fame now finally opening—thanks
largely to Pound—Joyce had published *Dubliners,* completed *A Portrait,* and, renewed by interest and support, begun writing *Exiles* and
Ulysses.

Yet as Pound prepared the literary world for Joyce's greatness, Europe turned its attention and concern to world war. Though in a
vulnerable position as foreigners, Joyce and his family managed to stay
in Trieste during the first year of hostilities but in June 1915 were
forced to leave when the military ordered a partial evacuation of the
city.[14] Eleven years after leaving Dublin Joyce and Nora fled, more as
refugees than exiles, with their two children to Zurich, the city that
had been their original destination in 1904.

Once in Zurich Joyce, also a genius at surviving personal adversity,
quickly found students for tutoring, made new friends, gathered new
debts, and profited from Pound's successful effort to find benefactors
interested in supporting Joyce's writing. With *Exiles* finished Joyce
turned to the business of finding a producer for the play, while he also
looked for someone to publish *A Portrait* in book form. Through the
effort of Harriet Weaver, coeditor of the *Egoist* and rapidly becoming
one of Joyce's most ardent supporters, *A Portrait* was published at the
end of 1916 by B. W. Huebsch, but the manuscript of *Exiles* was to

suffer the same difficulties as Joyce's other "Little Bo-Peep's sheep" before it found a home (*Letters*, 1:92).

With Europe at war and Ireland, after the Easter Rising of 1916, embroiled in its revolutionary Troubles, Joyce gave his attention to writing *Ulysses*. Even though attacks of glaucoma and synecchia threatened his eyesight and forced him to spend three months in Locarno, Joyce managed to send the completed *Telemachiad*—the first three episodes of *Ulysses*—to Pound by January 1918. Pound then quickly secured the *Little Review*, edited by Margaret Anderson and Jane Heap, for the serialization of *Ulysses*, which began with the publication of the first episode in the March 1918 issue.

With *Ulysses* launched and *Exiles* if not produced then at least published in May 1918, Joyce continued his writing to the point that the *Telemachiad* and four additional chapters were published in the *Little Review* by the end of 1918.[15] While Joyce completed the difficult middle chapters of *Ulysses* for serialization, he continued to struggle with serious eye problems and became embroiled in a legal dispute involving a member of an acting company for which in the previous year he had agreed to serve as business manager. Further frustrated by the poor reception of the first production of *Exiles* in Munich on 7 August 1919, Joyce decided to return with his family to Trieste but, now unhappy with his situation in the city he once regarded as his second home, was ready for another change and a new setting for the completion of *Ulysses*.

Just as Ezra Pound played steward to Joyce's writing, he now performed a similar role to the artist himself by convincing Joyce to live in Paris, where he would be in the eye of the modern literary world. While Joyce's own plan, when he arrived with his family in July 1920, was to visit Paris, he remained there until another world war would force him to move again. In Paris Joyce became a celebrity and a cause. New friends and apostles, aspiring and established writers, potential collaborators and even betrayers participated—some more eagerly than others—in the Joyce enterprise. What Joyce had forged and Pound had wrought was quickly becoming the stuff of controversy and even legend.

One such controversy that would add greatly to the legend of Joyce had been developing since the U.S. Post Office seized and destroyed four issues of the *Little Review* because of the *Ulysses* episodes.[16] When the government decided to prosecute the magazine's editors for publishing pornographic material, the American lawyer and patron of the arts John Quinn agreed to defend Anderson and Heap at their trial. An

active supporter of Joyce's work, Quinn, however, regarded the *Little
Review* as more interested in sensationalism than in art and defended
Anderson and Heap only because of his admiration for Joyce. After
Quinn moved unsuccessfully for a delay to give Joyce the time to finish
Ulysses and publish it in book form, the trial began on 14 February
1921. After several days Anderson and Heap were found guilty, fined
$50 each, and ordered to cease publication of *Ulysses* in the *Little
Review*.

With yet another of his works in jeopardy, Joyce once again was
rescued by an admirer willing to serve as apostle. Sylvia Beach, an
American expatriate and owner of the Shakespeare and Company bookstore in Paris, asked Joyce for the honor of publishing *Ulysses*. Once
Joyce accepted, other benefactors and supporters made arrangements to
publicize the book, while Harriet Weaver provided a list of possible
subscribers and agreed to publish an English edition of *Ulysses* under
the imprint of the Egoist Press. Overcoming severe eye pain and his
own frustrations with the last few episodes, Joyce managed to complete
Ulysses in time for the first copy to be placed in his hands on 2 February
1922, his fortieth birthday.

Finnegan

With *Ulysses* completed and published, Joyce had fulfilled his ambition of creating a literary masterpiece and had assured his own literary
immortality by producing the most influential novel of the twentieth
century. While *Ulysses* alternately captivated, disturbed, and offended
its readers, Joyce meanwhile had already begun to shape another book
in his mind.[17] In his 11 March 1923 letter to Harriet Weaver he
announced: "Yesterday I wrote two pages—the first I have written
since the final *Yes* of *Ulysses*" (*Letters*, 1:202).[18] As the literary world
tried to come to terms with *Ulysses*, Joyce turned to a new work that for
the next 16 years would occupy and drain his creative energies as well as
severely test the loyalty of his friends and supporters.

In the years after *Ulysses* Joyce would encounter more than the difficult task of writing *Finnegans Wake* and the growing resistance to his
"Earwicker absurdity" (*Letters*, 1:203). His diseased eyes and rotting
teeth demanded more and more attention to the point where furious
attacks of pain, near blindness, and frequent eye operations were among
the few predictable events for him in what was normally a hectic and
nomadic existence. Joyce persisted with the *Wake* in the face of the

judgments of Stanislaus Joyce, Harriet Weaver, Ezra Pound, and others that he was wasting his genius. He published the first fragment of the book in the April 1924 issue of Ford Madox Ford's *transatlantic review* in a literary supplement called *Work in Progress,* a title Joyce quickly seized on so that he could keep the actual title a secret and a mystery. Joyce, however, also faced his fifth and sixth eye operations in June and November 1924 and by April 1926, after a seventh operation, could read and write only with the aid of a magnifying glass.

While *Exiles* gave Joyce a measure of satisfaction when it was produced in New York in February 1925 and, a year later, in London, he suffered more distress, in addition to his tenth eye operation, when he learned that *Ulysses,* banned and not protected by copyright in the United States and England, was being pirated by Samuel Roth in *Two Worlds Monthly.* Even though Joyce organized the "International Protest," a document prepared by American writers Ludwig Lewisohn and Archibald MacLeish and signed by 167 scientists, philosophers, and artists,[19] Roth continued to serialize his bowdlerized version of *Ulysses* until finally stopped by a court injunction in December 1928.

Encouraged by a legitimate offer from new friends and ardent supporters Eugene and Maria Jolas to serialize his "Work in Progress," Joyce completed several more sections of *Finnegans Wake* and also had a small volume of poetry published as *Pomes Penyeach* in July 1927. During this period he continued the orchestration of his career and reputation by supervising the German and French translations of *Ulysses,* helping Stuart Gilbert with his book *James Joyce's "Ulysses,"* overseeing the publication of a collection of *Wake* essays called *Our Exagmination Round His Factification for Incamination of Work in Progress,*[20] and selecting Herbert Gorman, an American journalist, critic, and novelist, as his official biographer. In early 1930 Joyce also experienced some improvement in his eyesight after undergoing his eleventh operation, this one performed in Zurich by the Swiss surgeon Alfred Vogt.

Yet Joyce's slightly and temporarily improved vision and his persistence with the writing and publication of fragments of the *Wake* were overshadowed by other continuing problems—the Joyces' extravagant spending, their nomadic movement, their periodic bouts of poor health—and new problems with Georgio and Lucia. In their son's case the Joyces worried about the instability of his marriage to Helen Fleischman, an American woman 10 years his senior, and the uncertainty of his career as a singer. The former event prompted Joyce, worried about the legitimacy of his children and future grandchildren, to set up a temporary residence in England for the purpose of marrying Nora; the wedding, duly sensationalized by the press, took place in London on 4 July 1931.

Lucia's problems, apparently intensified by her brother's and her parents' marriages, were so serious that they exhausted and nearly overwhelmed the already erratic domestic and social existence of the Joyces in the 1930s. What over the years had been characterized as Lucia's odd behavior now deteriorated into madness. While Joyce endured the painful loss of his father, who died on 29 December 1931, and delighted in the birth of his grandson, Stephen, on 15 February 1932, he struggled against the increasing evidence of his daughter's schizophrenia. By early 1932 Joyce had developed a pattern of denial and false optimism, followed, usually after an incident of Lucia's violent behavior, by the decision to send her for a brief stay at a clinic or on an ostensible holiday with a member of the Joyce circle, either Harriet Weaver or Maria Jolas. Finally, after consultations with a variety of doctors, including Carl Jung, and after numerous transfers from clinic to clinic interspersed with disastrous visits to Ireland and England, Lucia was placed by her still-unbelieving father in a sanitorium in Ivry, a Paris suburb, in April 1936.

Ten years earlier Joyce had described *Finnegans Wake* as "my experiment in interpreting 'the dark night of the soul' " (*Letters*, 1:258). By 1937 he saw the completion of the *Wake* as a release from his own dark night. Despite the debilitating effects of his family problems, the frustration with friends over their failure to see the worth of his *Work in Progress,* and the resulting mental depression and continuing physical decline, Joyce remained obsessed with the *Wake* and hoped to finish it in time for a 2 February 1938 publication. He did not, however, write the celebrated last lines of *Finnegans Wake* until November 1938, and the book itself, though a copy was delivered to him in time for his fifty-seventh birthday, did not appear until May 1939.

Joyce had hoped that *Finnegans Wake,* which takes for its subject matter the entire range of human history and experience, would command no less than worldwide attention and controversy. The improbability, if not impossibility, of his expectation that readers would have lots of fun at *Finnegans Wake* was quickly evident, however, in the mixed and often-confused reviews of the book.[21] Even more depressing for Joyce was the growing realization that his 16-year creation was little more than an imp of the imagination compared with the monstrous approach of World War II. Just as in Joyce's view world war had complicated the writing of *Ulysses,* war now was to distract the world's attention from *Finnegans Wake,* which for its creator had become more real than anything else in his life.

Yet even Joyce could not avoid the sweep of the historical circumstances of his life. When the war began he reluctantly prepared, once again, to become a refugee. When remaining in Paris became impossible after the German occupation in June 1940, the Joyces moved to Saint-Gerand, a village near Vichy. As Joyce's health, complicated now by severe stomach pain, declined sharply, the Joyces rejected Maria Jolas's plea that they come to the United States and instead decided to return to Zurich, where they had spent the duration of World War I.

Overcoming great difficulties in securing permits, the Joyces managed to leave unoccupied France and, after brief stops in Geneva and Lausanne, arrived in Zurich on 17 December 1940. After barely a month of rest and seclusion Joyce was suddenly stricken with stomach pain. Suffering from a perforated ulcer, he underwent an operation immediately. Though the operation appeared successful his condition worsened, and, as Nora rushed to be with him, Joyce died in a Zurich hospital early in the morning of 13 January 1941.

The Wake

On 15 January 1941 James Joyce was buried with modest ceremony and decorations in a Zurich cemetery. His immediate legacy to his family was similarly sparse: his wife was isolated and without funds; his son had his own serious drinking problem and no career; and his daughter was in a sanitorium in German-held territory. The Joyce family, like its counterpart in *Finnegans Wake,* did, however, survive war and its aftermath and, at least in the case of Nora and Georgio, found a renewed life.[22]

A few years after the war's end the body of William Butler Yeats, who had died in the south of France in 1939, was returned with great honor and ceremony to Ireland for burial in his beloved County Sligo.[23] No such fate, however, awaited the body of James Joyce. Its only resurrection, unlike the ubiquitous form of HCE from the *Wake,* was a change of cemetery plot in 1966 so that Joyce and Nora, who had died in 1951, could be buried together.

As for Joyce's reputation, it soared again out of the ashes of war, as Joyce scholars, not unlike the enduring ALP of the *Wake,* gathered the bits and pieces—the manuscripts, letters, and other memorabilia—to put together once again the life and reputation of the most experimental and dominating writer of the twentieth century. While Joyce once declared that he was a writer of bitter memory and little imagination, the literary world for the most part would now remember him as a great artist and imaginative genius whose life became "the portals of discovery" (*U*, 156) through which he observed the consciousness and events of his age and reshaped them through his own vision into literary masterpieces.

Once, however, the first edition of Joyce's letters appeared in 1957, Joyce's life as reflected in his correspondence began to generate as much controversy as his art. Some reviewers found it hard to believe that the creator of *Ulysses* could have written such mediocre and disappointing letters. Others concluded that the 1957 volume exposed Joyce's failure or inability to see or reach out beyond his own needs and interests. Even Joyce, who declared his letters "full of materiality," could write self-mockingly about his desperate and pathetic efforts to keep career and family afloat: "at the fatal hour I appear at the door in dubious habiliments, with impedimenta of baggage, a mute expectant family, a patch over one eye howling dismally for aid" (*Letters*, 1:132, 197).

When two additional volumes of letters appeared in 1966, reviewers, disappointed by the earlier collection, found even more evidence of Joyce's cadging, self-advertisement, charlatanism, pedantry, and supreme arrogance. Lamenting the absence of a moral voice in Joyce's writings, Lionel Trilling saw the additional letters as further confirmation of Joyce's lack of humanity, his ferocious, absolute "commitment of himself to himself," and his grubbing desire for fame.[24] Disturbed by Joyce's frequent manipulation of his family to support his early ambitions and career, Anthony Burgess saw Joyce as a monster of a son and brother.[25]

Joyce's letters to Nora in the 1966 volumes, rather than moderating the harsh criticism of his personal life, merely added support—because of the letters' often infantile and perverse tone—to those now willing to think the worst of him. Readers became even more shocked and enraged, however, when two new Nora letters, exposing Joyce's sexual cravings and obscene fantasies, appeared in *Selected Letters*, published in 1975. This time reviewers went beyond condemning the letters to arguing whether they should have been published at all. While some wondered if readers would giggle or gag, Irving Howe, questioning the "moral and aesthetic appropriateness" of the letters to Nora, saw their publication as part of the "relentless undermining of privacy" that had become a "disturbing feature of American culture."[26]

Although the publication of Joyce's letters has provoked unhappiness, anger, and even disgust at this revelation of a private portrait of the artist, over the years the correspondence has also provided Joyce's readers with important keys in negotiating the labyrinth of his art and in understanding the personality behind the fiction. Some readers, in sharp contrast with reviewers who read Joyce's letters as the reflection of a lowbrow, coldhearted megalomaniac, have discovered an admirable human being in Joyce's devotion to Nora and the children, his courage in enduring personal and public adversity, his loyalty and gratitude to his supporters, his singular commitment to art, and even his sense of humor, especially his ability to laugh at himself. They have also found the correspondence to be a rich sourcebook for insights into his writing. Joyce's comments on his work, ranging from his defense of *Dubliners* to his explications of passages from *Finnegans Wake,* have become critical commonplaces and yielded a number of catchphrases for Joyce scholars. The reader of the letters discovers the youthful Joyce "up to the neck" in Aristotle; the companion of Nora noticing "how women when they write disregard stops and capital letters"; the frustrated artist declaring his "mouth is full of decayed teeth and . . . soul of decayed ambitions"; the lonely lover describing his letters as "ugly, obscene, and bestial" but also "pure and holy and spiritual"; the author of *A Portrait* and *Ulysses* claiming that he has "little imagination"; and the campaign manager for *Finnegans Wake* advising reluctant readers and friends that they should "not pay overmuch attention to these theories [of Bruno and Vico] beyond using them for all they are worth" and feeling reassured that "there are patient souls, who will wade through anything for the sake of the possible joke" (*Letters* 2:38, 173, 216, 249; 1:101, 241; 3:146).

Since the publication of the first volume of Joyce letters it has become apparent that readers looking for the best in Joyce have admired the courageous artist and dedicated family man living by perseverance and wit, while those suspecting the worst have discovered arrogance, alienation, and manipulation in Joyce's treatment of friends and family. In a sense the reaction to Joyce's letters runs parallel to the criticism of his major works, especially *Ulysses* and *Finnegans Wake.* Those looking for artistic mastery and comic vision have admired Joyce's craftsmanship and humor, while others anticipating artistic gamemanship and an emptiness of spirit have also been satisfied they have found their man. As for Joyce's vision or version of himself, he could easily play Stephen Dedalus for those who admired or worshiped the artist or Leopold Bloom for those who cared for the man. His favorite role, however, one also recognized by friends and critics, was that of a modern Job, suffering outrageous and undeserved setbacks but keeping faith, with the help of a little self-mockery, in his own genius and vision of himself as the artist.

Chapter Two
The Simplest Verbal Vesture: Lyrics and Epiphanies

In the final chapter of *A Portrait* Stephen Dedalus, attempting to define literary forms, claims that lyrical literature, which he describes as "the simplest verbal vesture of an instant of emotion" (*P*, 214), represents the artist's first attempt at imaginative expression. True to form, James Joyce's first artistic impulses inspired the lyrics that were eventually collected for *Chamber Music*, his first published book. While Joyce eventually doubted the honesty of *Chamber Music* and disassociated himself from the poems, in a letter written in February 1907 just a few months before the book's publication he admitted to his brother Stanislaus that "I have certain ideas I would like to give form to: not as a doctrine but as the continuation of the expression of myself which I now see I began in *Chamber Music*" (*Letters* 2:217).

After first meeting Joyce in 1920 Ezra Pound noted to John Quinn, "Joyce—pleasing; after the first shell of cantankerous Irishman, I got the impression that the real man is the author of *Chamber Music*, the sensitive. The rest is the genius; the registration of reality on the temperament, the delicate temperament of the early poems."[1] Pound's perceptive distinction between Joycean temperament and genius, helpful in understanding Joyce's transformation from the poet of the delicate verses of *Chamber Music* into the creator of masterworks of fiction, also points back to another distinct verbal form that cloaked Joyce's first imaginative expression. As Joyce expressed his "delicate temperament" in poetic form, he also used prose to record often-apparently-trivial moments that he described as epiphanies: "By an epiphany he meant a sudden spiritual manifestation, whether in the vulgarity of speech or of gesture or in a memorable phase of the mind itself" (*SH*, 211).

Borrowing the term from the Feast of the Epiphany, the church day celebrating the revelation of Jesus's divine nature to the Magi, Joyce turned theology into art by collecting from his Dublin youth moments of thought, dialogue, or narrative that had both spiritual and artistic value. Joyce's epiphanies, described by his brother Stanislaus as "manifestations or relevations" and by Oliver Gogarty as "any showing forth of the mind by which . . . one gave oneself away," more likely represent Joyce's first efforts to sketch the actual life of Dublin while recording the impressions made by these moments on the mind of the young artist.[2] Robert Scholes and Richard Kain point out that the epiphanies "should probably be thought of as a realistic, prose antithesis of the elegant verses of *Chamber Music*" (Scholes and Kain, 5). The brief sketches should also be read, however, as the early record of the prose genius that would eventually develop the observed and experienced moments of youth into the cold detachment of *Dubliners* and the impressionistic skill of *A Portrait of the Artist as a Young Man.*

Chamber Music

Like the lover in Ernest Dowson's Cynara poem, Joyce's critics have been faithful to *Chamber Music* in their fashion. Unwilling to abandon the poems entirely as the expression of Joyce's youthful temperament, they find more acceptable William York Tindall's view that *"Chamber Music* may be a minor work, but it is a minor work of a major writer."[3] For Tindall the poems should be taken seriously because they are, in their own fashion, faithful autobiographically to Joyce's youth, a view supportive of Pound's earlier judgment as well as expressive of Joyce's major themes and methods. Moreover, the poems merit their own critical attention because they are technically brilliant, if thin in substance; are richly derivative, echoing Elizabethan, romantic, and decadent verse; and, taken together, are evidently structured in narrative and symbolic form in a manner that resembles and foreshadows Joyce's prose works.

The seriousness of Joyce's youthful attitude toward the poems of *Chamber Music,* before his misgivings about their publication, expresses itself in *Stephen Hero,* the first draft of *A Portrait.* In this manuscript version of Joyce's autobiographical novel Stephen's characterization of the poet exposes the Joyce who wanted copies of his verses sent to the great libraries of the world in case of his early death and later prepared a parchment manuscript of *Chamber Music* as a gift for Nora:

To none of his former fervours had he given himself with such a whole heart as to this fervour; <<the monk now seemed to him no more than half the artist.

He persuaded himself that it is necessary for an artist to labour incessantly at his art if he wishes to express completely even the simplest conception and he believed that every moment of inspiration must be paid for in advance. He was not convinced of the truth of the saying [*Poeta nascitur, non fit*] 'The poet is born, not made' but he was quite sure>> of the truth of this at least: [*Poema fit, non nascitur*] 'The poem is made not born'. (*SH*, 32–33)

Rejecting the "burgher" notion of divine inspiration and proclaiming isolation as the artist's first principle, Stephen eventually decides to "make his scattered love verses into a perfect wreath," even though "he felt compelled to express his love a little ironically" (*SH*, 174).

In actuality Joyce's love verses, written in the manner of Elizabethan songs but mingled with a modern note, were apparently arranged into a wreath for *Chamber Music* by his brother Stanislaus, who had earlier suggested the title for the collection. While Joyce took great care in composing their delicate surface and precise sound, he became so disenchanted with his poems that he turned their arrangement for publication over to Stanislaus. In two letters written to Tindall Stanislaus explained that he had arranged the 36 poems in their present order "to suggest a closed episode of youth and love" and that his brother accepted the arrangement "without question and without comment" (*CM*, 44). He also noted that he hoped the poems would be read as a "connected sequence," or poetic narrative, of a closed chapter of his brother's "intensely lived life in Dublin" before going "into voluntary exile" (*CM*, 44).

According to the claims of Stanislaus Joyce, *Chamber Music* in its present arrangement expresses the instances of emotion, the aspirations and disappointments, that first inspire and later disillusion the poetic imagination. Read sequentially, Joyce's love verses also become the emotional counterpart, perhaps even the musical counterpoint, to the realistic stories of *Dubliners* in recording the temperament or emotional life of the poet as preliminary to narrating the hard circumstances of his youth. Apparently worlds apart in subject and style, *Chamber Music* and *Dubliners* are nevertheless precise renderings, in the manner Joyce found necessary, of the conditions that forced him into exile, while each book in its own fashion sounds the modern note preparatory to the eventual composition of his modern epic.

While *Chamber Music* opens with an allegretto, or lively suite of verses, appropriate to youthful hope and desire, the first poem has a more subdued and slower tempo, perhaps in anticipation of the down-

ward movement that closes the arrangement.[4] In poem I, Love personi-
fied wanders along the river as he listens to the "music sweet" made by
nature. With head bent in listening and in homage, Love tries to
compose upon the strings of his instrument notes correspondent to the
music played by nature's strings. Poem II creates a chordlike effect by
repeating the three quatrain and rhymed second and fourth line strategy of the first poem as the parallel, in effect simultaneous, image
emerges of the beloved listening, with head bent, to distant music
while her fingers stray upon the piano.

With lovers distracted from the common world by nature's strings
and drawn irresistibly toward each other by the music of night and, of
course, the musical imagery and composition of the opening verses,
poem III carries Love—once again on the strings of nature's harps—to
the threshold of sunrise and anticipated fulfillment. The next several
poems simply vary Love's attendance in song upon the beloved as lover
desires to enter his maiden's heart while at the same time celebrating
within the context of gay breezes and sunny woodland her virginal
qualities. By poems IX and X, Love, traveling a circuitous path, still
seeks the beloved but now confidently urges others to leave behind
their dreams and follow the heart's desire:

> And the time of dreaming
> Dreams is over—
> As lover to lover,
> Sweetheart, I come. (*CM*, 127)

After a similar entreaty for the beloved to "bid adieu" to her girlish
days and sentimental ways, "Happy Love" in poem XIII sends a message on the winds of "good courtesy" that the bridal wind is now
blowing and Love, now at his noon, will soon be with her. Poem XIV,
described by Joyce as central to his suite of songs, becomes climactic, as
some critics claim, if taken as the moment of awakening for the lovers
from youthful and virginal dreams to the world of real love. More Song
of Solomon than Elizabethan song, poem XIV, with the voice of Love,
directly appeals to the beloved to arise and go now, not to Innisfree but
to her lover's arms. In one of the more provocative moments in *Chamber
Music* the beloved, described in each of the poem's four stanzas as a fair
and beautiful dove, is urged through the further repetition of the word
arise to enter the woods where

> I wait by the cedar tree,
>   My sister, my love.
> White breast of the dove,
>   My breast shall be your bed. (*CM*, 135)

With Love now joined, the remaining poems in *Chamber Music*, after an interlude of celebration in which nature accompanies the awakening of the lovers, move steadily downward as Joyce's bower of bliss not surprisingly becomes entangled with human emotions. Joyce's love verses, no longer sweetly and shyly evocative, become testament to the emotional disillusionment and eventual failure that follows love awakened. Love's first casualty becomes friendship, as successive poems (XVII–XIX) acknowledge the unwitting pain inflicted on friends by Love's self-absorption and Love's own sorrow at friends' deceit and envy that follow this innocent betrayal.

Scorned by friends, Love becomes so completely isolated within the beloved's companionship that he gladly sees himself detained by the "sweet imprisonment" of her arms. Self-doubt, however, soon undermines this delicate security and emotional dependency as Love, sensing the vulnerability and temporality of his happiness, gently chides his beloved in poem XXIV for neglecting him because of her own self-absorption:

> The sun is in the willow leaves
>   And on the dappled grass,
> And still she's combing her long hair
>   Before the looking-glass. (*CM*, 155)

With the heart now presaging woe, Love urges the beloved in poem XXV to sing joyfully even when "the heart is heaviest," but even within the "soft choiring of delight" heard by the beloved in poem XVI and presumably sung by Love there lurks a sound that makes the "heart to fear." This fearful sound, even though Love can still turn the beloved's head with the "elegant and antique phrase" so characteristic of the love verses in *Chamber Music*, is Joyce's modern note, identified as the deceit or malice that hides in the tenderest of loves celebrated by the poets:

> Nor have I known a love whose praise
>   Our piping poets solemnize,
> Neither a love where may not be
>   Ever so little falsity. (*CM*, 161)

Now weary of ardent ways, Love seeks comfort in the song "about the long deep sleep / Of lovers that are dead" (*CM*, 163). Unfortunately, Love must first endure the wild and desolate winds—in contrast to the gentle breezes that first awakened Love—that are harbingers of the complete dissolution of happiness and desire. Poem XXX then offers the striking image of Love and the beloved as "grave lovers" now that time's "sweet hours" are gone and "Love is past" (*CM*, 167).

While poems XXX and XXXI appear to offer another interlude, they appeal merely to the memory of summer's soft breath, after desolate winds, and the beloved's sweet kiss, after Love's dying fall. The impossibility of Love's return becomes clear in poem XXXIII where the imagery of whistling winds and falling leaves points toward parting lovers, the end of the year, and the closing of Love's song:

> Now, O now, we hear no more
> The vilanelle and roundelay!
> Yet will we kiss, sweetheart, before
> We take sad leave at close of day.
> Grieve not, sweetheart, for anything—
> The year, the year is gathering. (*CM*, 173)

All that remains in *Chamber Music* is poem XXXIV, described by Joyce as "vitally the end of the book," and two additional poems serving, according to Joyce, as "tailpieces" to his "suite of songs" (*Letters*, 1:67). Joyce's end song gently and appropriately urges the "unquiet heart" to sleep, but the winter wind, correspondent and ironic companion to the troubled heart, cries "Sleep no more." While poem XXIV concludes Joyce's suite with Love giving one last kiss to the beloved in the hope of granting her a final measure of peace and quiet, the last two poems acting as tailpieces, or a coda, offer no such rest for Love, who now appears more poet than personification. In poem XXXV, the poet, apparently embarked on his journey into exile, finds companionship only in the sad and lonely seabird and correspondent song in the cold wind and flowing sea. Poem XXXVI, greatly admired by Ezra Pound,[5] then closes *Chamber Music* with the nightmarish but nevertheless stirring image of armed warriors so blinding in their fury that the poet becomes defenseless against their power: "My heart, have you no wisdom thus to despair? / My love, my love, my love, why have you left me / alone?" (*CM*, 179).

The final powerful image in *Chamber Music* of the exile devastated by the raging vision of his own imagination fits the general critical judgment of Joyce as the poet: that the early poems mark both a beginning and a point of departure for Joyce from the thin lyrical voice limited by an inherited style to the modern artist capable of epic range and dramatic distance. In this essential transition and transformation from temperament to genius or from young man to artist Joyce never abandoned his first love, but his later poetry was written either within the context of his vast fictional world, such as "The Villanelle of the Temptress" in *A Portrait*, or on the occasion of a major emotional event in his life, such as the greatly admired "Ecce Puer," written after the death of his father and the birth of his grandson. After *Chamber Music* Joyce's poetic gift, strengthened by his feeling that the gift had been betrayed by those closest to him, served to give him the precision and authority needed to write the imaginative history of his people, first as moral chapter and autobiographical experience but eventually as mythic adventure and visionary dream.

Dubliners

Joyce as a young man barely survived the near decade of frustration, disappointment, and discouragement in finding a publisher for *Dubliners*, but Joyce the artist staunchly defended the book against its detractors. One of his most important pronouncements is contained in a 5 May 1906 letter to Grant Richards in which Joyce responded to the printer's complaints about "Two Gallants," certain passages in "Counterparts," and the use of the word *bloody* in "Grace." After justifying both the language and the content of his stories, Joyce offered his much-quoted explanation and defense of his purpose and method in writing *Dubliners:*

My intention was to write a chapter of the moral history of my country and I chose Dublin for the scene because the city seemed to me the centre of paralysis. I have tried to present it to the indifferent public under four of its aspects: childhood, adolescence, maturity, and public life. The stories are arranged in this order. I have written it for the most part in a style of scrupulous meanness and with the conviction that he is a very bold man who dares to alter in the presentment, still more to deform, whatever he has seen and heard. I cannot do any more than this. I cannot alter what I have written. (*Letters*, 2:134)

This statement of intention, arrangement, and method has heavily influenced the critical study of *Dubliners,* especially by providing key catchphrases for interpreting the stories and understanding the design of the collection itself. Joyce's comment on intention, that he chose Dublin as the setting for his chapter on Ireland's moral history because the city seemed the center of paralysis, has provided focus and credibility for thematic studies of *Dubliners.* By selecting the city as moral center, Joyce, in Florence Walzl's words, "embraced intuitively the great modern theme of the city, at the very beginning of an age of world cities and universal mass culture."[6] In revealing the paralysis within Dublin of the Irish citizen, Joyce further grasped the commonality of the moral, emotional, and spiritual paralysis afflicting Dublin life and the necessity, at least for the artist, to escape from the restrictive conventions or nets of family, country, and religion: "I will not serve that in which I no longer believe whether it call itself my home, my fatherland or my church" (*P,* 246–47).

The young artist's cry of freedom in *A Portrait* remains, however, a book removed from the trapped chorus in *Dubliners.* In his letter to Richards Joyce also stated his specific intention of revealing the paralysis of his Dubliners at four representative levels of human generation and enterprise. Before composing his portrait of the artist Joyce, with an uncompromising and unrelenting vision, had hoped to create individual studies that would take shape in the reader's mind as a broad spectrum of human nature trapped by parochialism and self-doubt. Just as Joyce attempted to weave the texture of each story into the composite structure of *Dubliners,* he wanted each painful case to signify a larger truth for the modern reader.

This larger truth, however, is balanced in *Dubliners* by the exactness of execution. While Joyce's statements on intention clearly emphasize the representative and structural importance of the stories, his defense of the language of *Dubliners* and his comments on its style also point to the precision and objectivity of narration. Though *Dubliners* has symbolic intentions, each story has narrative integrity. The language and style of *Dubliners,* scrupulous to the point of apparent meanness in exposing and detailing the desperate lives of its characters, aspire to the artistic impersonality that Gustave Flaubert defined as the principle by which art creates the appearance of reality and a vision or at least the illusion of truth: "It is one of my principles that a writer should not be his own theme. An artist must be in his work like God in creation, invisible and all-powerful; he should be everywhere felt, but nowhere seen. Furthermore, Art must rise above personal emotions and nervous susceptibilities. It is time to endow it with pitiless method, with the exactness of the physical sciences."[7]

Yet the method of *Dubliners,* unalterable even in a word according to Joyce because of the exactness of its observations and the integrity of its revelations, also has about it a "special odour of corruption" (*Letters,* 1:123). While each story artfully and objectively exposes the paralysis of the individual character within a broad pattern of Dublin life, the very narrative of the book becomes infected or corrupted by the failed life of each Dubliner. As Joyce wrote to Richards, "It is not my fault that the odour of ashpits and old weeds and offal hangs round my stories. I seriously believe that you will retard the course of civilization in Ireland by preventing the Irish people from having one good look at themselves in my nicely polished looking-glass" (*Letters,* 2:63–64).

For many readers Joyce's "nicely polished looking-glass" offers illumination as well as a reflection of character. While noting that none of Joyce's 40 surviving epiphanies actually appear in *Dubliners,* certain critics have not hesitated in assuming the importance of the concept of the epiphany to Joyce's stories. Morris Beja, for example, contends that "*Dubliners,* which does not include a single passage based on any of the surviving epiphany manuscripts, is sprinkled with sudden revelations for its protagonists or illuminating fragments of life for its readers. In Joyce, it can be no mere coincidence that after all the slices of life and evanescent moments of the sketches throughout the volume, the climactic revelations in the final story, 'The Dead,' all occur on Twelfth Night—the Feast of the Epiphany."[8] Beja's comments reveal the tendency of critics who read the stories as epiphanies to divide the revelations in *Dubliners* into two categories: those which awaken a character's consciousness of his or her particular condition of paralysis and those which illuminate the text for the reader even though Joyce's character often prefers, even demands, the dark: "No, damn it all, said Mr. Kernan sensibly, I draw the line there. I'll do the job right enough. I'll do the retreat business and confession, and . . . all that business. But . . . no candles! No, damn it all, I bar the candles!"[9]

Joyce introduces the fictive world of *Dubliners* with three childhood stories told from the first-person point of view of the child. This narrative strategy of using the apparently innocent eye to observe the first manifestations of paralysis in *Dubliners* creates a deceptive simplicity for the reader. By narrating the opening stories from the child's perspective Joyce gains an immediacy and directness of experience,

especially through the child's voice and language, as well as the detachment and objectivity necessary to achieve the imaginative sense of
reality and truth prescribed by Flaubert. The innocent eye observes,
records, and even reacts to an event but as yet is incapable of distorting
reality because of its own shortsightedness. Yet this eye is not immune
from infection from the diseased condition it observes: "Every night as I
gazed up at the window I said softly to myself the word *paralysis*. It had
always sounded strangely in my ears, like the word *gnomon* in the Euclid
and the word *simony* in the Catechism. But now it sounded to me like
the name of some maleficent and sinful being. It filled me with fear,
and yet I longed to be nearer to it and to look upon its deadly work" (*D*,
9). This passage from the first page of "The Sisters," the opening story
in *Dubliners*, yields the word *paralysis*, thereby marking the collection's
major theme, within the narrative context of a young boy's anticipation
of the death of an old priest following the priest's third stroke. The
words *gnomon* and *simony* also provide critical markers for the reader,
who will soon learn of Father Flynn's strange befriending of the young
boy and the incompleteness of the priest's life.[10] This information
comes to the reader as the boy, once learning of the priest's death,
remembers his friendship with Father Flynn and records the comments
made by adults about the priest's unfortunate life.

   As the boy listens to the adults he receives a series of impressions that
give credibility to his confused feelings and his own haunting image of
the priest. At supper the boy hears Old Cotter, a friend of the family,
say that there was "something queer . . . there was something un-
canny" (*D*, 10) about Father Flynn and that the boy should not have
spent so much time with the old priest, because children's "minds are
so impressionable. When children see things like that, you know, it has
an effect" (*D*, 11).

   The next morning the boy discovers that he feels a sensation of
release or freedom, but his memories of his time with Father Flynn
actually increase the underlying, even insidious sense in "The Sisters" of
something queer or wrong, something yet to be confessed. As the boy,
realizing that he should be mourning Father Flynn's death, recalls the
wondrous things he had been taught by the old priest, the reader learns
that these lessons had much to do with the mysteries of the Church.
During the boy's visit, Father Flynn had made him learn the responses
of the mass, had instructed him on the meaning of the mass and the
different vestments worn by the priest, and had even questioned him on
the difference between venial and mortal sins and mere imperfections.

When the boy's thoughts circle back to his dream, he remembers details that reveal how the teachings of Father Flynn have had a subtle and strange influence on his mind: "I remembered that I had noticed long velvet curtains and a swinging lamp of antique fashion. I felt that I had been very far away, in some land where the customs were strange." (*D, * 13–14).

While the boy cannot remember the end of his dream, the reader still has one more opportunity to learn more about the waking nightmare of Father Flynn's life that has so disturbed the adult world. In the evening the boy and his aunt attend the house of mourning and, after saying their prayers for the coffined priest, visit with Father Flynn's sisters. The desired confession is now impossible, but the boy becomes the medium for the reader by listening attentively to the sisters' revealing comments about their brother's failure—that "too scrupulous always" in his duties as a priest, he became "a disappointed man" (*D, * 17). In particular, the boy hears and the reader learns that, after accidentally breaking a chalice, Father Flynn, his mind affected by the incident, was found sitting alone in the confession box: "Wide-awake and laughing—like to himself. . . . So then, of course, when they saw that, that made them think that there was something gone wrong with him" (*D, * 18).

In "The Sisters" Joyce's narrative does not allow the reader to become privy to the secret thoughts of Father Flynn. The priest's attempts at confession remain inaccessible to the sisters and incomprehensible to the young boy. While learning that there was something wrong, some failure in Father Flynn's spiritual life correspondent to his physical paralysis, the reader never comes in direct contact with the true nature or source of the priest's condition. The effect of Joyce's strategy, then, is to place both narrative and thematic emphasis on the ambiguous yet insidious influence of the adult world on the mind and soul of the child. If there is an epiphany in Joyce's opening story, it comes in the revelation that what the boy sees and hears has already begun its corrupting effect and that even the most innocent of Joyce's characters is not safe from the paralysis of Dublin life.

In the remaining two children's stories Joyce repeats the narrative strategy of the first-person point of view but alters the reader's perception of the paralysis in *Dubliners* by making the corruption of the adult world more directly evident and eventually internalized within the child himself. "An Encounter" begins innocently as a schoolboy tale of two youths out for a day of truancy. Bored with reading wild West stories and playing childhood games, Joyce's youthful narrator seeks an escape from the routine of school in the world of real adventures. What he encounters with his friend, however, is far beyond the range of his own expectations and the romantic adventures of pulp fiction.

After wandering about most of the day and failing to reach their goal of the Pigeon House, the boys meet a man who at first seems merely odd.[11] Once the man is alone with the story's narrator, the "queer old josser" shifts his "liberal" inquiries about the boy's sweethearts to a compulsive, sinister monologue on whipping young boys who have sweethearts and lie about it: "He described to me how he would whip such a boy as if he were unfolding some elaborate mystery" (D, 27). No more capable of understanding his direct encounter with perversion than the boy in "The Sisters" could comprehend the failed life of the priest, Joyce's youth in "An Encounter" penitently turns back to his friend's companionship even as the circle of corruption and the condition of paralysis move closer and closer to the heart of innocence.

In "Araby" the youthful heart is finally stricken, though at first glance the problem seems little more than the stuff of romance. Joyce's childhood narrator, now obviously approaching adolescence, is even wearier of school and games and, not yet old enough to be weary of ardent ways, seeks escape in his infatuation with Mangan's sister. His call to adventure comes when Mangan's sister—whose name, never given in the story, is celebrated in secret prayer—informs the devoted youth that she cannot go to Araby, a local bazaar, because she is required to attend a retreat. Promising like a knight-errant to bring her something from Araby, the youth discovers, once he gets to the bazaar and fails to find a gift, the foolishness of his promise and his quest: "I saw myself as a creature driven and derided by vanity; and my eyes burned with anguish and anger" (D, 35).

After the oppressive atmosphere of the paralytic in "The Sisters" and the direct contact with the pervert in "An Encounter," Joyce offers an image of anger and impotence in "Araby" that closes out his childhood stories and encloses their young narrators within a circle of spiritual, moral, and emotional frustration and failure. While commentators, intrigued by the potential epiphany revealed in the last statement of "Araby," have debated how much the narrator comprehends about the source of his vanity, the narrative of Joyce's last childhood story takes its central consciousness to a stage of awareness and development preparatory for the next four stories of adolescence.[12] Once this shift occurs, however, the perspective in *Dubliners* changes from the eye of the child, temporarily protected by its own innocence, to the eye of the observer, protected and necessarily limited by its detachment from the general condition.

The change in point of view that begins in *Dubliners* with the four stories of adolescence also marks a transfer in focus from the innocent child threatened by the paralyzing corruption of adult life to the immature adult unable to escape that paralysis even though the condition is clearly perceived and understood. In "Eveline," for example, a 19-year-old woman knows that ever since her mother's death her own life has become increasingly unbearable, that it promises nothing but household drudgery, hard work, and the likelihood of physical abuse from her drunken father. Knowing that if she stays in Dublin she will repeat her mother's life—"that life of commonplace sacrifices closing in final craziness" (*D,* 40)—Eveline recognizes that her only hope for happiness is to run away with her lover, Frank. When the moment of departure comes, however, Eveline's sense of duty to her family and her fear of the unknown prevent her from leaving: "She set her white face to him, passive, like a helpless animal. Her eyes gave him no sign of love or farewell or recognition" (*D,* 41).

"Eveline," one of Joyce's most beautifully crafted stories in its creation of the paralytic's drab existence and passive nature, is followed by "After the Race," generally regarded as the weakest story in *Dubliners.*[13] Its young paralytic experiences the sensation of adventure and freedom because of the international character of his race-car companions and the financial backing of his father, but the illusory nature of his experience becomes evident in his lack of sophistication and his reckless play at cards. While the fast pace and crowd in "After the Race" make the story an odd fit in a collection of narratives marked by drab settings and stagnated lives, Jimmy Doyle nonetheless clearly belongs with Eveline Hill and the Joycean adolescents to follow in their failure to seize the opportunity for a new life free of Dublin's paralysis.

In "Two Gallants" and "The Boarding House" Joyce expands his circle of failed adolescents to include the 30-year-old Lenehen, a notorious Dublin leech, and the 34- or 35-year-old Mr. Doran, a respected employee in a Catholic wine-merchant's office. These apparent opposites further illuminate the condition of paralysis by extending the world of adolescence from young adulthood to approaching middle age, thereby acknowledging the difficulty if not impossibility in *Dubliners* of ever attaining the maturity, fulfillment, and happiness commonly associated with a successful adult life. In the process Lenehan and Doran also expose, with their own moral and emotional timidity and acquiescence, the growing vulnerability of Joyce's characters to the unscrupulous, brutal side of Dublin life.

In Lenehan Joyce draws one of his most chilling portraits in *Dubliners* of failed sensibility. Lenehan has intelligence and awareness but uses his cleverness and eloquence merely to survive as "a sporting vagrant armed with a vast stock of stories, limericks, and riddles" (*D*, 50). In "Two Gallants" the reader observes Lenehan's latest maneuvering as he stays close to Corley, a bully and braggart intent on getting money from a young servant girl. While Corley goes about his business with his "tart," Lenehan, wandering the Dublin streets, hopes for a better and happier life with his own "good simple-minded girl with a little of the ready" (*D*, 58). When Corley, gold coin in hand, reveals his success, Lenehan, his ravaged life already evident in his appearance, knows that at least on this night his leeching will yield a successful night of drinking and stories in the company of his fellow gallant.

In "The Boarding House" Mr. Doran—the title of respect bestowed ironically on him by Joyce—appears, unlike Lenehan, to be the model of success with his position in the wine-merchant's office, his attendance to his religious duties, and his regular life. Nevertheless, he proves himself to be another case of arrested development, no further advanced emotionally in his vulnerability to flirtation than the boy in "Araby." The momentary anguish and anger felt by Joyce's youth, however, count little compared with the fear and trembling experienced by Mr. Doran when he realizes he is trapped by Mrs. Mooney's anticipated demand for the only reparation possible for the recovery of her daughter's honor. While his instincts, like those of Eveline, warn him to flee the situation, Mr. Doran, recognizing the threat of scandal and worse, knows he will yield to Mrs. Mooney and marry her daughter. The reader is not a party to the moment of accounting between Mrs. Mooney and Mr. Doran, but the otherwise-painfully-blunt narrative of "The Boarding House" leaves little doubt about the future of Joyce's last adolescent.

Joyce follows "The Boarding House" with his four adult stories, but any anticipation or illusion that marriage may be the rite of passage into a meaningful and fulfilling life is quickly dispelled in "A Little Cloud" and "Counterparts." Like Mr. Doran, Little Chandler, described as "a neat modest figure" (*D*, 71), appears reasonably adjusted, successful, and even refined, but the contrast between his undersize physical stature and his condescending attitude gives away the true nature of his adult character. Though Chandler imagines himself above the common horde because of his poetic nature, in actuality he works in a tiresome clerical position, lacks the courage and commitment to write verse, and finds himself trapped by marriage and parenthood. When he shares a few drinks with Ignatius Gallaher, an old crony and now a self-proclaimed successful London journalist, Chandler recognizes, in the contrast between Gallaher's bold, independent manner and his own timid, petty existence, that he is "a prisoner for life" (*D*, 84). This revelation leads, however, only to Chandler's momentary panic and abusive anger against his infant son and is quickly followed by feelings of shame and remorse.

In "Counterparts" Joyce presents Little Chandler's apparent opposite in the bulky Farrington, yet this second look at the adult married Dubliner reveals the same condition of paralysis no matter what the temperament. Unlike Chandler, Farrington fancies himself a man among men, feels only too comfortable in a bar, and has a way with words, even to his detriment. His heavy drinking, however, makes his position as a scrivener and his family life intolerable. After jeopardizing his job with a smart answer to the chief clerk, Farrington pawns his watch for a night of drinking, only to spend his money without becoming drunk and to lose his reputation as a strongman when defeated in arm wrestling by a younger man. Filled with fury he returns home and, like Chandler, takes out his frustration on his child. While timid and poetic Chandler merely shouts at his infant son, Farrington, more brutish and violent, beats his son with a stick as the poor child's only hope of escape rings out with a hollow irony at this stage in *Dubliners:* "Don't beat me, pa! And I'll . . . I'll say a *Hail Mary* for you . . . I'll say a *Hail Mary* for you, pa, if you don't beat me . . . I'll say a *Hail Mary*" (*D*, 98).

With married life exposed as the prison house for his adult Dubliner, Joyce turns to the unmarried adult in "Clay" and "A Painful Case." Maria, a literary sister of Little Chandler in her diminutive body and her disappointed shyness, has been condemned to spinsterhood by her unattractive, witchlike appearance and because of a family quarrel is now forced to live and work in a laundry run by Protestants. On All Hallows' Eve she visits the family of one of her brothers for an evening of treats and entertainment, but the narrative of "Clay," while capturing the polite naïveté of Maria's character, remains scrupulous in observing the meanness of the life imposed on her.[14] The trick played on her by the children—substituting a lump of garden clay for the blindfolded Maria to choose in their game of divination instead of the traditional water, ring, or prayer book—foreshadows the bleak future of this Dubliner closed off from travel, marriage, and even the atmosphere of family and religion. Her omission of the second stanza of "I Dreamt That I Dwelt" and its lines about suitors on bended knees, though regarded as a mistake by her family, is final evidence of the pain of Maria's life, just as her brother Joe's tearful search for the corkscrew betrays his true condition and the bitter reality behind the simple and polite narrative of "Clay."

James Duffy, Maria's unmarried counterpart in *Dubliners,* hardly qualifies as a victim. Unlike Maria, Duffy has carefully plotted his life into a well-ordered "adventureless tale" (*D,* 109). Cold and skeptical, Duffy has developed a detachment comparable to Joyce's early epiphanies and the narratives of *Dubliners* itself: "He lived at a little distance from his body, regarding his own acts with doubtful side-glances. He had an odd autobiographical habit which led him to compose in his mind from time to time a short sentence about himself containing a subject in the third person and a predicate in the past tense" (*D,* 108).

When a brief friendship with a married woman, Mrs. Sinico, threatens to become an emotional and moral entanglement Duffy abruptly ends the relationship before it becomes an affair. Four years later, when he reads of the vulgar circumstances of Mrs. Sinico's accidental death, he immediately feels vindicated in his decision not to involve himself with a woman who had turned to drink at the end of her life. Momentarily revolted by the narrative of her death, Duffy soon, however, begins to recognize his responsibility for her loneliness and death and for his own isolation, now more a condemnation than a choice, from love and happiness. In one of the most stunning epiphanies in *Dubliners* Duffy awakens to the painful truth about his buried life: "No one wanted him; he was an outcast from life's feast" (*D,* 117).

After this final revelation of the hidden meanness, emptiness, and loneliness of his adult Dubliners Joyce turns to public life with three stories that show how the condition of paralysis has further corrupted Ireland's politics, culture, and religion. "Ivy Day in the Committee Room," with its gallery of petty political canvassers and its nicely polished reflection of the shallow deceit of Dublin politics, stands as Joyce's favorite story in *Dubliners*. Joyce's canvassers parade into the committee room, only to inflate their own efforts, question the loyalty and integrity of others, and belittle their own candidate for this by-election, ironically held on the anniversary of Charles Stewart Parnell's death. Only when the promised bottles appear do Joyce's canvassers become fraternal and supportive in their remarks, even extending their generosity to the English king. With spirits rising in accord with the alcoholic fumes that force the corks out of the heated bottles, all that remains is for Joe Hynes, the one Parnell loyalist, to evoke the spirit of the dead chief with a recitation in his honor. Hynes's poem, little more than doggerel though accurate enough in its condemnation of the cowards and hypocrites who betrayed Parnell and now sit in audience, sounds the closing note on a politic life so lacking in honesty, decency, and commitment that loyalty is bought for a bottle and genius is mocked even when the mocker is most sincere.

"A Mother," Joyce's close study of Dublin's cultural community, is placed perfectly after "Ivy Day in the Committee Room." After an unforgiving view of local politicians still willing to betray, Joyce attends to the Irish Revival, which filled the vacuum in Dublin's public life after the scandal and fall of Parnell. Joyce's hard look in "A Mother" at the mediocrity of the artists and organizers of the moment, however, contrasts sharply with Yeats's vision of an Ireland liberated culturally and intellectually after centuries of political failure.

In "A Mother" the most striking and disturbing characteristic of the Dublin cultural community, besides its lack of talent and genius, is its blatant desire to use the arts for financial, social, or political gain. Mrs. Kearney, eager to manipulate the concert's organizers for her daughter's benefit, is little more than a shallowly cultivated and domestically secure version of Mrs. Mooney in "The Boarding House." When the concert and its organizers fail to live up to her expectations, Mrs. Kearney also expresses, in her rage, the same frustration with her buried life and the same tendency toward emotionally explosive and violent behavior that characterize Joyce's married adults in the earlier stories.

After exposing the commonplace corruption and petty betrayals in Irish politics and culture, Joyce completes his mosaic of Dublin life with a story on religion. Any possibility, however, that the Catholic Church has the cure for the paralysis afflicting Joyce's *Dubliners* has already been undermined, beginning with "The Sisters," at every level or aspect in the collection. "Grace," with its focus on a retreat for businessmen, is simply Joyce's most detailed and symbolically structured look at the failure of religion in the lives of his characters and their own lack of spiritual vision or understanding.

Tom Kernan's fall down the stairs of a Dublin bar begins a three-level narrative in "Grace" that parallels the divisions of hell, purgatory, and paradise in Dante's *Divine Comedy*. At the first level, the reader finds Kernan, drunk, injured, and deserted by his drinking companions, descended into the filth and slime of a basement lavatory. From this hellish state Kernan, a commerical traveler by profession, rises from his fallen condition and journeys back to his home for a period of recovery and repentance. While recovering he is visited by four business associates who, in their effort to bring Kernan back to a state of public grace, or respectability, convince him to attend a retreat with them. Although Kernan attends the retreat and completes his journey from the bowels of a Dublin bar through a period of recovery in his own bed to a state of renewed respectability, the retreat itself offers a mock-paradise that barely hides its true purpose. Once the priest begins to speak, however, the convenient, practical, and mutually beneficial arrangement between the Church and the business community becomes painfully apparent: "He came to speak to business men and he would speak to them in a businesslike way. If he might use the metaphor, he said, he was their spiritual accountant" (*D*, 174).

After the failure of politics, culture, and religion, the major narrative event of "The Dead"—the "Morkan's annual dance," celebrating the Christmas season and apparently held on the night of the Epiphany—represents the last hope in *Dubliners* for release or escape from the condition of paralysis. As discouraging as the title of "The Dead" appears to be, some Joyce critics have actually found a redeeming quality in the hospitality so much in evidence and duly celebrated by Gabriel Conroy in his after-dinner speech: "I feel more strongly with every recurring year that our country has no tradition which does it so much honour and which it should guard so jealously as that of its hospitality" (*D*, 202). Ellmann goes so far as to state that Gabriel Conroy's speech "was Joyce's oblique way, in language that mocked his own, of beginning the task of making amends" (Ellmann, 245).

Believing that "The Dead," in making amends, expresses Joyce's admiration for the Irish way of life and that the snow covering Ireland symbolizes Irish mutuality and connectedness, Ellmann describes the last story in *Dubliners* as Joyce's "first song of exile" (Ellmann, 253) and a love song at that. The narrative of "The Dead," however, seems to undermine this binding spirit of hospitality, just as the array of characters at the dance often appear as painful reminders of paralytics in earlier stories. In several minor scenes and small conversations, such as the recurring talk about the Church, the same vulgarity, narrow-mindedness, hypocrisy, and even drunkenness revisit *Dubliners* at this showcase of Dublin's social life. The occasion and intention of the event may be commendable, but the dance is attended by characters whose failed lives are barely concealed by the surface gaiety.

The insidiousness of the failed life is most evident in Gabriel Conroy, probably the most successful and respectable of Joyce's characters in *Dubliners.* Seemingly secure in his career and marriage, Gabriel from the beginning is unnerved by small but distracting incidents that also provide the reader with echoes from previous narratives. Lily's bitter complaint—that men are all palaver—to Gabriel's playful suggestion that she should be married soon discomposes Gabriel but also rings out as a reminder of Corley's betrayal in "Two Gallants," particularly when Gabriel gives Lily a coin to smooth things over. Other incidents, especially the prickly exchange with Miss Ivors, the ardent nationalist, further disturb Gabriel's composure, but they too offer further echoes of the already-sounded limitations of Irish adulthood and public life. Even politic Gabriel, when pressed by Miss Ivors to learn more about the Irish way of life, retorts, "I'm sick of my own country, sick of it" (*D,* 189).

Gabriel's epiphany, his moment of illumination into his own buried life, comes after he mistakingly believes that Gretta, his wife, has been stirred by the evening's events, including his successful after-dinner speech, into a rekindled passion for him. Fired by this conviction Gabriel unfortunately discovers, once they leave the dance and arrive at their hotel room, that his wife has instead been aroused by a song that has reminded her of Michael Furey, a Galway youth. Years before, he had died of his love for Gretta by standing in the cold rain, despite his delicate health, after learning that she was leaving for convent school. Emotionally devastated by Gretta's revelation, Gabriel suddenly gains insight into the folly of his own actions: "He saw himself as a ludicrous figure, acting as a pennyboy for his aunts, a nervous, well-meaning sentimentalist, orating to vulgarians and idealising his own clownish lusts, the pitiable fatuous fellow he had caught a glimpse of in the mirror. Instinctively he turned his back more to the light lest she might see the shame that burned upon his forehead" (*D,* 220).

After Gretta falls asleep, Gabriel, possessed by such terrible knowledge, feels his own existence fading as his soul moves closer to the region of the dead. Realizing that the snow, "general all over Ireland," has begun to fall again, he envisions it snowing on the lonely churchyard grave of Michael Furey and, as Gabriel's own soul slowly swoons, "upon all the living and the dead" (*D*, 224). While it is possible to read this final image as a symbol of mutuality and connectedness, the falling snow more likely becomes the final reminder of the paralysis general all over Dublin in a collection of stories that begins with the statement "There was no hope" and ends with the words "the dead."

Chapter Three

A Fluid and Lambent Narrative: Portrait of the Artist

In his discussion of literary forms in the last chapter of *A Portrait*, Stephen Dedalus envisions the expression of the artist's personality, "at first a cry or a cadence or a mood," progressing into "a fluid and lambent narrative" (*P*, 215). Having at first expressed his own personality within the delicate moods and cadences of his lyrics, Joyce soon turned, even as he composed his early verse, to the writing of prose pieces or epiphanies. As he developed these simple sketches into the complex stories of *Dubliners* Joyce also made his first attempt at expressing the artist's personality in "the rhythms of phrase and period" with his narrative essay "A Portrait of the Artist." In the essay he defined a portrait as "not an identificative paper but rather the curve of an emotion" and declared the artist independent of "the general paralysis of an insane society."[1]

Shortly after completing "A Portrait of the Artist," Joyce decided to expand his essay—which had been rejected for publication—into an autobiographical novel. The surviving manuscripts of Joyce's preliminary text, which he titled *Stephen Hero*, show that he originally intended to write a novel significantly longer than and different from *A Portrait of the Artist as a Young Man*. As Theodore Spencer points out in his introduction to the published edition of *Stephen Hero*, the early version of Joyce's autobiographical novel "portrays many characters and incidents which the published version leaves out, and it describes the growth of Stephen's mind in a far more direct and less elliptical form than that which we are familiar" (*SH*, 10). The early version also treats more extensively Stephen's interest in aesthetic theory, including his explanation and illustration of his concept of epiphany.

Perhaps the most interesting revelations in the surviving manuscript fragments of *Stephen Hero* come from the scenes, not included in *A*

Portrait, involving members of the Dedalus family barely glimpsed or mentioned in the novel's final form. There are several scenes, for example, between Stephen and his brother Maurice, obviously modeled after Joyce's brother Stanislaus, and a dramatic series of scenes involving the illness and death of his sister Isabel. Even more interesting to Joyce readers are the conversations between Stephen and his mother, including the argument over Easter duty merely reported by Stephen in *A Portrait;* In *Stephen Hero,* however, the scene is vividly portrayed:

—I never thought I would see the day when a child of mine would lose the faith. God knows I didn't. I did my best for you to keep you in the right way.

Mrs. Dedalus began to cry. Stephen, having eaten and drunk all within his province, rose and went towards the door:

—It's all the fault of those books and the company you keep. Out at all hours of the night instead of in your home, the proper place for you. I'll burn every one of them. I won't have them in the house to corrupt anyone else.

Stephen halted at the door and turned towards his mother who had now broken out into tears:

—If you were a genuine Roman Catholic, mother, you would burn me as well as the books. (*SH,* 135)

Since most of the *Stephen Hero* fragments cover Stephen's university days, it is not surprising that the surviving manuscript also offers additional materials on Stephen's aesthetics, including the often-quoted definition of epiphany. The *Stephen Hero* manuscript, for example, includes not only an early version of Stephen's discussion of lyrical, epical, and dramatic art and the three stages of aesthetic apprehension but a sharp distinction between the romantic and classical voices and a definition of the modern spirit. Rejecting the "heroic, the fabulous" art of the romantic for "the slow elaborative patience" (*SH,* 97) of the classical temper, Stephen uses his definition of the modern spirit as "vivisective" (*SH,* 186) to correct the tendency of the "lantern of tradition" to "transform and disfigure" (*SH,* 186). In his talks with Maurice, Lynch, and Cranly Stephen also has much more to say about the smothering effect of Catholic education on the minds and spirits of the university students: "I found a day-school full of terrorised boys, banded together in a complicity of diffidence. They have eyes only for their future jobs: to secure their future jobs they will write themselves in and out of convictions, toil and labour to insinuate themselves into the good graces of the Jesuits. They adore Jesus and Mary and Joseph:

they believe in the <<infallibility>> of the Pope and in all his obscene, stinking hells: they desire the millennium which is to be [a] the season for glorified believers and fried atheists" (*SH, 232*).

Stephen Hero has provided important material for the scholar interested in Joyce's development as an artist, but the student reader of *A Portrait of the Artist as a Young Man* should consider Thomas Connolly's advice that *Stephen Hero* "be among the last of the Joyce texts for a student of Joyce to approach because it is a fragment and an unfinished text at best."[2] When Joyce transformed his working draft into a modern novel, he dramatically cut its shape and altered its focus. Having painted with "scrupulous meanness" the landscape and supporting cast of his fiction in *Dubliners,* he now created within that environment a portrait of Irish genius so finely carved and crafted that Ezra Pound praised the finished novel as "hard, perfect stuff."[3]

Yet Joyce's own genius devised a narrative strategy whereby he balanced this hardness of portraiture, achieved primarily through the use of irony, with an impressionistic vision of Dublin life reflective of the developing consciousness of the young artist. Through the compound lens of impressionism and irony Joyce recorded the artist's personality within "a fluid and lambent narrative" of such permanent value that Pound placed Joyce, at this stage in his career, between Thomas Hardy and Henry James in the development of the modern English novel (Pound, 319).

A Portrait of the Artist as a Young Man

The first page and a half of *A Portrait of the Artist as a Young Man* may surprise the reader expecting the unrelenting, impersonal narrative of *Dubliners.* The novel begins with "Once upon a time" and follows this time-honored incantation of the storyteller with a brief series of sharp impressions of Stephen Dedalus's early life narrated in the language of a young child. Yet the opening of *A Portrait* achieves an effect similar to the first page of *Dubliners* by setting out critical markers for the reader, who will trace the artist through five phases of youthful development.

While some critics have described the beginning paragraphs of *A Portrait* as an elaborately designed matrix or microcosm for the novel, the more general view finds in Stephen's first impressions the awakening of his five senses to the world's delights, expressed in story, song, and dance, and its dangers, expressed in bodily discomfort and the threat of punishment for disobedience.[4] The opening sequence of events, however, also identifies either directly or indirectly the key relationships and influences in Stephen's early life as well as the small child's sensitivity to language and the arts. Though the first line of *A Portrait* places its narration within the great tradition of storytelling and anticipates the religious and mythic implications—also evident in Stephen's name—of the artist's mission, the opening paragraphs further suggest the modernity of the novel's style and structure. Joyce's portrait will reveal Stephen's development not only through his special but limited perspective but in a language and structure fitting for each chapter or stage until Stephen discovers his calling: "To live, to err, to fall, to triumph, to recreate life out of life" (*P,* 172).

It is not surprising, considering the autobiographical nature of *A Portrait,* that the key to the criticism of the novel's narrative has been the personality of Stephen Dedalus and Joyce's attitude or distance from that personality.[5] While the novel's title clearly claims a special genius or vocation for Stephen—that of artist—but modifies that genius by tracing and fixing it at a particular stage of development—as a young man—critics have often preferred to choose between "the artist" and "the young man" in their judgments of Joyce's intention.

Those who read the novel as a portrait of artistic genius usually sympathize with Stephen's ordeals, approve his aesthetic theories, and see him overcoming the treachery of his Dublin youth as he flies into voluntary exile to write his masterpiece.[6] Those who read *A Portrait* as an ironically conceived apprenticeship novel find only a young man and condemn Stephen's arrogance, mock his aesthetics as self-defensive, and judge him as hopelessly immature, a case of arrested development despite his lofty claims. Hugh Kenner has been especially vigilant in debunking Stephen, describing him as a fake artist, "indigestibly Byronic," and as the spiritual brother of the broken or resigned failures in *Dubliners.*[7]

This critical debate over Stephen's personality and potential has also influenced the study of the narrative form of *A Portrait.* Sympathetic readers have plunged into the novel's impressionistic flux only to see that flux as an actual process of becoming, out of which Stephen finally emerges as the artist-creator of his own life. Less sympathetic readers have remained aloof from the narrative's impressionism and have seen the novel as an ironic demonstration of the failure of talent or genius, while judging Stephen as an incurable product of his environment, his generation, and his own sensibility.

Some readers, sensing an unresolvable tension between the novel's impressionism and its irony, make the claim for a double vision forming the narration of *A Portrait*. This view accommodates both Joyce's identification with Stephen and his detachment from the narrative of his autobiographical hero. Unfortunately, since these readers emphasize how Joyce perceives his own novel and its self-proclaimed hero, they have trouble deciding whether Joyce's final portrait is one of understanding, tempered by irony, or irony, softened by compassion. In any case the same dilemma or enigma—the conflicting virtues and vices of Stephen's personality—also haunts those who perceive both an admirable and a dislikable central character but cannot decide where Joyce places his final emphasis.

Considering the impressionistic style and language of *A Portrait*, the critical emphasis on the character of Stephen Dedalus seems reasonable and justifiable, but a close study of the narrative itself offers another perspective. As Stephen advances impressionistically through the stages of crisis or development that Ellmann compares to "the gestation of the soul" (Ellmann, 297), the narrative of *A Portrait* moves according to its own rhythm. In other words Stephen's perceptions give a definite though varying form to the chapters of *A Portrait*, but the narrative also records a reality external to Stephen's vision and thoughts that is both visible and audible to the reader.

The narrative of the first chapter in *A Portrait* focuses on the first major crisis in the development of the artist as he begins to move toward the discovery of his true nature and mission. Through three episodes of Stephen's early life the reader witnesses Stephen's tentative, confused attempts to adjust to the world around him. All three events, however—his illness after being pushed by Wells into the square ditch, the political quarrel at the Christmas dinner table, and the pandying from Father Dolan—disrupt the order of things despite Stephen's efforts, most evident in his writing on the flyleaf of his geography book and in his fascination with words, to understand his proper place in the universe: "It was very big to think about everything and everywhere. Only God could do that" (*P*, 16).

In the Clongowes episodes Stephen's confusion is a physical phenomenon for him, because his vision is disturbed and distorted first by his bout with the "collywobbles" and then by the accidental breaking of his glasses. Only when Stephen tells the rector about the "unjust and cruel and unfair" (*P*, 53) pandying and is assured that the rector will speak to Father Dolan is the focus of authority restored, at least in Stephen's impressionable young mind. The experiences, though temporally disruptive, also, however, begin a pattern of doubt, suspicion, and hostility that will lead a rebellious Stephen to his fateful decision to reject the priesthood of the Roman Catholic Church and become a priest of art.

While Stephen's painful experiences at school and home appear to shift back and forth abruptly in the first chapter, the narrative has its own definite pattern and achieves a symmetry ironically appropriate to Stephen's naive quest for order and reason in the midst of the insidious, irrational rhetoric and behavior of his older schoolmates, priests, and family. Though there is a gap of several months between each episode, the narration maintains a sense of continuity as it moves ineluctably from season to season, and a sense of balance as Stephen's ordeals begin and end at Clongowes.

The first narrative impression of Stephen's school days is cloaked in the gloom of early October 1891. Stephen, "caught in the whirl of a scrimmage" (P, 9), anticipates changing the number pasted inside his desk from 77 to 76 (the days remaining before the holiday) and dreams of Parnell's body being returned to Dublin.[8] In the second episode the narrative advances to Christmas, the holiday anticipated at Clongowes, as the scene dramatically shifts to Stephen's first Christmas Day dinner at his father's table, where the political content of the quarrel reinforces the earlier vividness of Parnell's death in Stephen's mind. In the final episode, the second at Clongowes, Stephen shares in the general atmosphere of fear at the school but he also notices that the boys are preparing for cricket. After suffering the fright, pain, and shame of the pandying, Stephen, filled with a sense of the act's injustice, finds that he cannot eat his Lenten meal. Only after Stephen's visit to the rector and his jubilant return to his schoolmates does the world at Clongowes appear to return to its normal order, now measured by the mockingly gentle sound of the cricket bats: "pick, pack, pock, puck: like drops of water in a fountain falling softly in the brimming bowl" (P, 59).

Thus as the seasons advance from fall to winter to spring Stephen undergoes three disturbing experiences that momentarily bewilder his sense of the proper order of things, until the rector tells him that Father Dolan's "mistake" will be corrected: "I shall speak to Father Dolan myself. Will that do now?" (P, 57). Yet Stephen's happiness and his restored faith in authority—expressed in his innocent determination to be "very quiet and obedient" (P, 59)—have already been been corrupted by his encounters with the bullying and cowardice of his schoolmates, the fiery political rhetoric delivered against the Irish priests for betraying Parnell, and the seemingly arbitrary act of cruelty and abuse administered by the prefect of studies. These events, appearing within a seasonal pattern that establishes an early sense of inevitability to the narrative of *A Portrait,* have started the young boy toward the moment of his epiphany and his eventual decision to seek exile as the artist's condition and defense.

After the thrill of his premature flight in the "cradle" made by the hands of his schoolmates, Stephen may happily return for a time to the cloak of obedience, but the narrative in *A Portrait* advances to the next crisis in his youthful development. Through another sequence of disturbing and painful impressions, Stephen, after his ordeal with the authority figures surrounding his childhood, must struggle with the impulses of his own body. Thus Stephen undergoes a fitful adolescent journey—from his romantic dreams of Mercedes through his frustrations with his feelings for E—— C—— and finally to his first sexual experience with the prostitute—that is also apprehended within a clearly visible movement of the seasons and by a dramatic change in language and narrative form appropriate to the advancing tide of puberty:[9] "How foolish his aim had been! He had tried to build a breakwater of order and elegance against the sordid tide of life without him and to dam up, by rules of conduct and active interests and new filial relations, the powerful recurrence of the tides within him. Useless. From without as from within the water had flowed over his barriers: their tides began once more to jostle fiercely above the crumbled mole" (*P,* 98).

At the beginning of the second chapter Stephen, now several years older, feels the first stirrings of sexuality. As he becomes increasingly skeptical about the adult world, he, like the boy in "Araby," is first drawn into his own romantic fantasies. While the gradual decline in his family's fortunes acts as "so many slight shocks to his boyish conception of the world," he pores over his ragged translation of *The Count of Monte Cristo* and awaits the "magic moment" when he will "meet in the real world the unsubstantial image which his soul so constantly beheld" (*P,* 65).

Still years away from his transformation into the artist, Stephen now suffers through all the weakness, timidity, and inexperience of the adolescent. Angered by his father's troubles and his own youth, he does shift the attention of his confused emotions from the imaginary heroine of a romantic novel and the Eileen of his childhood experiences, only to fail when Emma flirts with him on the tram. The next day, however, he responds imaginatively to his infatuation and her flirtation by composing a poem, his first expression of juvenilia, to E—— C——: "Some undefined sorrow was hidden in the hearts of the protagonists as they stood in silence beneath the leafless trees and when the moment of farewell had come the kiss, which had been withheld by one, was given by both" (*P*, 70–71).

The poem, written by Stephen but, unlike the later villanelle, not given in the narrative, is obviously a pale representation of the actual encounter: "There remained no trace of the tram itself nor of the trammen nor of the horses: nor did he and she appear vividly" (*P*, 70). Yet the verses mark a shift in perception of his imagined destiny—a shift apparently reflective of his developing emotional state—from romantic avenger to sorrowful lover. When he finally attends Belvedere, after his family's financial woes prevent him from returning to Clongowes, Stephen defends Byron as the greatest poet, even though his choice of the rebellious exile leads to another painful beating, this time from three schoolmates who brand Stephen and Byron as heretics.

Though Stephen briefly returns to the innocent apparel of boyhood by sharing in the "common mirth" of the Whitsuntide play, his frustration after his performance as the farcical pedagogue further indicates the increasing intensity of his emotions. His discovery that Emma, now clearly the object of his secret desires, has not stayed after the play jars his nerves and increases the riot in his blood to the degree that only the rank odor of animal urine and rotted straw can calm him. The narrative of *A Portrait,* however, allows the reader no pause as it leaps forward to the next critical event in Stephen's adolescent ordeal.

When Stephen visits Cork with his father to attend the auction of his family's remaining property, he undergoes an experience that brings into sharp focus—even for Joyce's confused adolescent—the emotional distance he has traveled since his days at Clongowes. In the anatomy theater at Queen's College Stephen, who now claims detachment from the adult world he once respected and feared, reads the word "*Foetus*" carved into one of the desks and suddenly discovers a trace in the outer world of what has now become his brutish malady: "The letters cut in the stained wood of the desk stared upon him, mocking his bodily weakness and futile enthusiasms and making him loathe himself for his own mad and filthy orgies" (*P*, 91).

Stephen judges his adolescence as a sickness or madness and believes that his childhood has since faded out of existence. With his romantic dreams usurped by masturbatory fantasies and the squalor of his life increasing as his father's fortunes continue their decline, Stephen, frustrated in his efforts to bring some semblance of the old order and elegance to his family life with his exhibition and essay prize money, finally turns to satisfying "the fierce longings of his heart" and "the savage desire within him" (*P*, 98). He prowls the Dublin street that once held the promise of a holy encounter, but now Stephen, caught in "the wasting fires of lust" (*P*, 99), seeks the company of a prostitute. When, however, he wanders into Dublin's nighttown, the narrative, increasing in intensity as Stephen circles closer and closer to his moment of sexual surrender, records the approaching event in a language appropriate to his extraordinary vision and the commonness of the experience itself.

Stephen's perception of his first sexual encounter is veiled in religious imagery—"yellow gasflames arose before his troubled vision against the vapoury sky, burning as if before an altar" (*P*, 100)—but the words spoken by the prostitute—"Good night, Willie dear" (*P*, 100)—cut through the emotional vapor, but only for the reader. When Stephen finally receives the long-denied yet -imagined kiss, he feels that the prostitute's lips "were the vehicle of a vague speech; and between them he felt an unknown and timid pressure darker than the swoon of sin, softer than sound or odour" (*P*, 101).

By the end of the second chapter Stephen has experienced two major crises, and his young life has advanced several years in the process. In both chapters he appears to resolve his ordeals, but his solutions, evident in his Icarus-like soaring and swooning, are merely premature and temporary. Instead, the narrative movement of *A Portrait,* while reflecting in its shifting structure and impressionistic language the changing nature of Stephen's struggles and stages of development, carries him inevitably to his crucial moments of discovery and decision. Before he reaches these climactic events of his youth Stephen, however, already alert to the dangers of the world around him and the demands of his own body, must now awaken to a crisis of the soul.

At the beginning of the third chapter Stephen, recovered from his earlier swoon, has nevertheless fallen into a state of complete sinfulness: "From the evil seed of lust all other deadly sins had sprung forth" (*P*, 106). Though increasingly aware of his soul's jeopardy, he at first feels indifferent to both his sins and the threat of damnation. When, however, he learns of the approaching retreat at Belvedere in honor of Saint Francis Xavier, Stephen's heart in dreadful anticipation withers up "like a flower of the desert that feels the simoom coming from afar" (*P*, 108). Since Stephen's spiritual crisis unfolds during the few days of the religious retreat, there are no great chronological leaps or fitful narrative moments in the third chapter. Most of the chapter's events take place from Wednesday, when Father Arnall begins his fiery sermon, to Saturday, the feast day of Saint Francis, celebrated on the third day in December. On the feast day itself Stephen, who begins the retreat in mortal fear for his soul, receives Holy Communion and believes he has overcome the monstrous urgings of his body by returning in spirit to the innocence of boyhood: "Another life! A life of grace and virtue and happiness! It was true. It was not a dream from which he would wake. The past was past" (P, 146). In the third chapter, then, as the narrative appears to slow down and the seasonal movement seems to pause at its darkest moment, Stephen experiences his own dark night of the soul but resolves his spiritual crisis by returning to the security and authority of the rituals of the Catholic Church.

Any possibility that Stephen's return to his childhood faith will permanently give substance and shape to his future has already been undermined by earlier narrative episodes, such as the unfair pandying at Clongowes and the rector's later betrayal of confidence in relating the story to Stephen's father: "when I told them all at dinner about it, Father Dolan and I had a great laugh over it" (P, 72). Further undermining Stephen's belief in his new spiritual life, however, is the very sermon that compels him to confess his sins and amend his daily life. Though completely effective in bringing Stephen back into the fold, the sermon is so nightmarish in its narration that Stephen becomes sickened and terrified rather than inspired by what he hears.

Because it dominates the narrative, Father Arnall's sermon on death, judgment, hell, and heaven also ironically imposes on the third chapter a tight structure based on the teaching of Ignatius Loyola, founder of the Jesuit order. In his *Spiritual Exercises* (1562) Loyola established a formal meditative procedure for those attending a religious retreat. Father Arnall's sermon adheres to this procedure, which requires the penitent to go through three stages: memory, or composition of place; understanding; and will. In following the first stage the sermon composes a vivid, physical vision of hell in which each of the five senses is tortured eternally: "Every sense of the flesh is tortured and every faculty of the soul therewith: the eyes with impenetrable utter darkness, the nose with noisome odours, the ears with yells and howls and execrations, the taste with foul matter, leprous corruption, nameless suffocating filth, the touch with red hot goads and spikes, with cruel tongues of flame" (P, 122). In its second stage the sermon then asks the schoolboys to understand the spiritual torments, especially the painful loss of family, friends, and God, that will accompany the physical torture of hell. Only at the very end of the sermon does Father Arnall allow the boys a moment to express their will by repeating the act of contrition.

Yet as the sermon compels Stephen to confession, communion, and a new life, it also undermines the Church's temporary victory over his soul because of the harshness of Father Arnall's rhetoric. In his determination to return his "dear little brethren" to a state of grace Father Arnall creates a portrait of a God that is so unrelenting and unforgiving in his pursuit and punishment of sinners that the old priest, near the end of the sermon, pauses to explain that "sin, be it in thought or deed, is a transgression of His law and God would not be God if He did not punish the transgressor" (*P,* 133). Thus, Lucifer, expressing "an instant of rebellious pride of the intellect," falls from glory, and Adam and Eve, after "an instant of folly and weakness," are driven out of Eden into a world of "death and suffering" (*P,* 134). But Stephen, terrorized at the moment into fear and self-loathing, will eventually and proudly declare his willingness, as the artist, to err and fall and his unwillingness to serve home, fatherland, or church or to fear being alone.

At the beginning of the fourth chapter Stephen's life is still dominated by his new religious regiment as he measures his days by the Church calendar: "Sunday was dedicated to the mystery of the Holy Trinity, Monday to the Holy Ghost, Tuesday. . . ." (*P,* 147). Yet despite his spiritual vision of the world as "one symmetrical expression of God's power and love" and his scrupulous and mortifying religious habits, he soon discovers that "the insistent voices of the flesh" are like "a flood slowly advancing towards his naked feet." Contemplating surrender, he waits "for the first faint timid noiseless wavelet to touch his fevered skin" (*P,* 152).

After a prelude devoted to the gradually fading rhythm of Stephen's amended life and the approaching call to a new adventure, the narrative of the fourth chapter abruptly leaps to the first of two significant moments of decision. Having struggled through distinct stages of development that have defined the nature of his environment as well as his own body and soul, Stephen now enters a climactic period in his life in which he will decide his vocation and mission. This stage, reflected structurally in the chapter by two sharply contrasting scenes and choices involving the priesthood, brings Stephen to a state of revelation and ecstatic release: "His soul was soaring in an air beyond the world and the body he knew was purified in a breath and delivered of incertitude and made radiant and commingled with the element of the spirit" (P, 169).

Stephen's moment of deliverance, though cloaked in the language of spiritual transformation, is not, however, in response to his recovered religious life. Although his first summons does come in the form of an opportunity to become a priest, Stephen knows that even though he has long contemplated the secret knowledge and power of the priesthood he will reject the director's offer because of his shadowy memories of Clongowes, his instinctive dread of the "chill and order" of the religious life, and his reviving pride of spirit: "He would never swing the thurible before the tabernacle as priest. His destiny was to be elusive of social or religious orders" (P, 162).

In making his exhortation the director asks Stephen to pray to his patron saint, Saint Stephen. The irony of this solemn appeal is that Stephen's second call, which comes as he waits impatiently for confirmation that he will enter the university, is first heard in a bantering of his name. The shouts of the bathers, however, rather than reminding Stephen of his saintly namesake, provoke an image out of the sound of his strange last name of "the fabulous artificer" of Greek mythology. This image of "a hawklike man flying sunward above the sea" then becomes for Stephen a prophecy of his destiny: "He would create proudly out of the freedom and power of his soul, as the great artificer whose name he bore, a living thing, new and soaring and beautiful, impalpable, imperishable" (P, 170).

Inspired by an image of his mythical forebear, Stephen affirms his true vocation and mission, but his confirmation as "priest of eternal imagination" comes moments later in a radiant vision of beauty. Feeling his soul finally liberated from "the grave of boyhood," he wades in a rivulet left by the receding tide until he encounters a girl who appears "like one whom magic had changed into the likeness of a strange and beautiful seabird" (P, 171). Her magical image, created out of the virgin womb of Stephen's own imagination, becomes both an epiphany and a call to adventure: "Her eyes had called him and his soul had leaped at the call. To live, to err, to fall, to triumph, to recreate life out of life! A wild angel had appeared to him, the angel of mortal youth and beauty, an envoy from the fair courts of life, to throw open before him in an instant of ecstasy the gates of all the ways of error and glory" (P, 172). As the radiance of Stephen's vision dims he feels his soul swooning once again, but this time rather than falling into sin it appears to unfold itself in a Dante-inspired dream of beauty and light:

"Glimmering and trembling, trembling and unfolding, a breaking light, an opening flower, it spread in endless succession to itself, breaking in full crimson and unfolding and fading to palest rose, leaf by leaf and wave of light by wave of light, flooding all the heavens with its soft flushes, every flush deeper than the other" (*P,* 172).

In the final chapter of *A Portrait* the narrative, now that Stephen's climactic discovery of his soul's potential has faded out, again alters its structure and mode to accommodate Stephen's next ordeal. Instead of radiating with the language of Stephen's previous state of rapture, the concluding narrative opens bleakly and ironically by exposing the continuing poverty and immaturity of his young manhood. In the first scene Stephen's vision cannot cloud over the squalor and disorder of the Dedalus home. Only when he departs for the university and is temporarily free from the offending voices of his family does he find relief from his misery and bitterness in remembered lines from Hauptmann, Newman, Cavalcanti, and Ibsen.

Stephen's earlier belief that his entry into the university would end the servitude of his boyhood and begin a new adventure for his liberated spirit has not, however, been fulfilled by the actuality of university life. While his mind searches for the essence of beauty in the writings of Aristotle and Aquinas, Stephen, still struggling with self-doubt and self-mistrust, finds the daily routine of his classes irrelevant, his teachers contemptible, and his youthful companions potential or actual betrayers. He regards his "monkish learning" as archaic to contemporary life, Irish culture as incapable of expressing itself in "a line of beauty," the Irish soul as batlike in its "darkness and secrecy and loneliness," and the English language in which he will express himself as the artist as "an acquired speech" imposed upon him by Ireland's conqueror (*P,* 180–89).

The narrative of chapter 5, after recording the initial thrusts of Stephen's rebelliousness, eventually takes its shape from a series of encounters in which Stephen either dismisses the ideas and advice of those around him or imposes his views on those still willing to tolerate him. The key encounters occur in counterbalancing conversations, first with Lynch, Stephen's intellectual sounding board, and then with Cranly, his spiritual confidant. These scenes, critical to Stephen's decision to leave Ireland, are punctuated by a brief moment when Stephen, his soul awakening to a morning inspiration, writes his villanelle to a temptress.

Before his important discussion of aesthetics with Lynch Stephen moves through three verbal exchanges that expose his intellectual pride and arrogance, but within a context charged with religion and politics. Having earlier rejected the priesthood, he now condescendingly dismisses the dean of studies and his speculations on beauty because Stephen feels that the priest's character is lacking in religious joy and passion. The words of this "poor Englishman in Ireland" still, however, wound Stephen's own spirit: "The language in which we are speaking is his before it is mine. How different are the words *home, Christ, ale, master*, on his lips and on mine! I cannot speak or write these words without unrest of spirit" (*P,* 189).

Offended by the director's manner, nationality, and ignorance, Stephen, after idly attending his physics class, goes from a strained but courteous exchange of ideas to a "war of wits" over his refusal to sign a petition in support of Czar Nicholas II's rescript for general disarmament and universal peace. Brushing aside Stephen's efforts at cynicism and indifference, MacCann attacks Stephen for hiding behind metaphors and provokes an angry response, nevertheless expressed metaphorically, that challenges the legitimacy of Nicholas's appeal. Once free of MacCann, Stephen endures one further indignation when he is scolded by Davin for his excessive pride and for turning his back on Ireland's cultural revival and its political struggle for freedom. When asked if he is Irish at all, Stephen, remembering past betrayals of Irish leaders, calls Ireland "the old sow that eats her farrow," after first declaring, as if to all his inquisitors, that "when the soul of a man is born in this country there are nets flung at it to hold it back from flight. You talk to me of nationality, language, religion. I shall try to fly by those nets" (*P,* 203).

After a quick series of confrontations the narrative shifts to a long discourse on aesthetics as Stephen wanders the Dublin streets with Lynch. Stephen's aesthetics—the centerpiece for the critical controversy over his character and Joyce's intent and achievement in *A Portrait*[10]—begins with a discussion of the tragic emotion: "a face looking two ways, towards terror and towards pity" (*P,* 205). Already stung by voices reminding him of the threats from family, religion, and country, Stephen, looking for a way of distancing himself and his art from emotional entanglement, next defines dramatic or aesthetically pleasing art as static because it arrests the mind and raises it above emotions and kinetic or improper art as pornographic or didactic because it excites the emotions of desire or loathing: "Beauty expressed by the artist cannot awaken in us an emotion which is kinetic or a sensation which is purely physical. It awakens, or ought to awaken, or induces, or ought to induce, an esthetic stasis, an ideal pity or an ideal terror, a stasis called forth, prolonged and at last dissolved by what I call the rhythm of beauty" (*P*, 206).

Using "the rhythm of beauty" as his aesthetic keynote, Stephen now moves on to a definition of art as "the human disposition of intelligible or sensible matter for an esthetic end" and a definition, borrowed from Aquinas, of beauty as the apprehension of that "which pleases" (*P*, 207). To understand the relationship between art and beauty, then, is to comprehend the nature of the imagination and the act of aesthetic apprehension because "the most satisfying relations of the sensible must therefore correspond to the necessary phases of artistic apprehension" (*P*, 211).

Borrowing from Aquinas once again, Stephen defines his "necessary phases of aesthetic apprehension" as *integritas, consonantia,* and *claritas,* which he translates as wholeness, harmony, and radiance. According to Stephen, the mind's eye experiences *integritas,* or the first phase of apprehension, when it perceives the aesthetic image as one thing in space or time, thereby recognizing both its wholeness and its separateness from everything it is not. This "synthesis of immediate perception" is followed by "the analysis of apprehension," or the process by which the mind apprehends the thing as "complex, multiple, divisible, separable, made up of its parts, the result of its parts and their sum, harmonious" (*P*, 212). After *consonantia* the mind clearly apprehends the radiant beauty of the aesthetic image: "the mind which has been arrested by its wholeness and fascinated by its harmony" enters a "luminous silent stasis of esthetic pleasure, a spiritual state" (*P*, 213).

Having established stasis as the governing principle of art, beauty, and the imagination, Stephen, judging literature as the highest art, now categorizes literary forms to suit his own need for emotional control and detachment. He designates the lyric as the simplest literary form because it expresses "an instant of emotion, a rhythmical cry" (*P*, 214). Once the artist turns from mood to thought, however, his personality passes into a narrative form in which he "broods upon himself as the centre of an epical event" (*P*, 214). To reach the final phase of aesthetic development, the artist, after expressing himself in the lyric and the epic, must impersonalize himself in the dramatic form: "The esthetic image in the dramatic form is life purified in and reprojected from the human imagination. The mystery of esthetic like that of material creation is accomplished. The artist, like the God of creation, remains within or behind or beyond or above his handiwork, invisible, refined out of existence, indifferent, paring his fingernails" (*P*, 215).

The narrative shift from Stephen's aesthetic discourse to his composition of the villanelle may appear as a logical progression in the last chapter of Joyce's portrait of the artist, but the scene, rather than illustrating Stephen's aesthetics, actually draws further attention to his youth and immaturity. Though enchanted and inspired by his dream of seraphic life, Stephen composes a poem that, while technically correct and impressive, clouds over his confused feelings for Emma by transforming her into the eternal temptress and his own doubting soul into one of the fallen seraphim. While he completes the villanelle to his own satisfaction, the painful and frustrating interruptions of recent memories and the sounds of the awakening life still surrounding him are far more revealing of the tumultuous emotional and spiritual condition of Stephen's young manhood than the vaporous words of the villanelle.

In the last major episode of *A Portrait* Stephen seeks out Cranly, who has already heard a number of "ardent, wayward confessions" (*P*, 232), to unburden himself after an unpleasant quarrel with his mother over his refusal to perform his Easter duties. In sharp contrast to his earlier confession at the religious retreat Stephen's emotional exchange with Cranly reveals his fears more than his sins, leads to an act of declaration rather than contrition, and anticipates not the Holy Communion of his mother's religion but the time when, as "priest of eternal imagination," he will transmute "the daily bread of experience into the radiant body of everyliving life" (*P*, 221). Stephen's statements to Cranly also reinforce his defiant rejection of "that in which I no longer believe whether it call itself my home, my fatherland or my church" and his ardent determination to express himself "in some mode or life or art as freely as I can and as wholly as I can, using for my defence the only arms I allow myself to use—silence, exile, and cunning" (*P*, 247).

With Stephen now firmly set in his decision to leave Ireland, the narrative concludes with a series of final thoughts, recorded as diary entries, that parallel the opening impressions of the novel. While Stephen's early impressions anticipate the direction and events that will shape his youth, his diary entries try to close out his youth by dismissing the past and brooding on the future: "The past is consumed in the present and the present is living only because it brings forth the future" (*P*, 251). His last two entries, anticipating his departure from Ireland, end the novel with a reaffirmation of his vocation and mission—"I go to encounter for the millionth time the reality of experience and to forge in the smithy of my soul the uncreated conscience of my race"—

and a final prayer to his mythical forebear—"Old father, old artificer, stand me now and ever in good stead" (*P*, 253).

Like the Daedalus of Ovid's *Metamorphoses*, Stephen too has set his mind to work upon unknown arts, but the ironic mode of the last chapter of *A Portrait* and Stephen's arrogant rejection of everyone and everything around him suggest that he, like Icarus, is not yet ready for the reality of experience or capable of forging radiant images in the smithy of his soul. The narrative does, however, record the actuality of Stephen discovering his essential nature or soul within the experience of his youth, as well as the potentiality in Stephen, evident in his temperament and genius, for creating the uncreated conscience of his race. Because Joyce's novel is a portrait of the artist as a young man, the reader does not see, except in the form of the novel itself, the mature expression of the artist. Nevertheless, the achievement of *A Portrait of the Artist as a Young Man* shows that when the artist has genius and maturity he can give a special and universal meaning to his own nature, transmute the daily bread of his experience into ever-living life, and grant the reader a feast day—or a Bloomsday perhaps.

Chapter Four

No Longer Purely Personal: Ulysses on Bloomsday

In his further delineation of literary forms Stephen Dedalus sees the epic emerging out of lyrical literature when the artist "broods upon himself as the centre of an epical event" (*P*, 214). At first the simplest of forms, the epic progresses until "the centre of emotional gravity is equidistant from the artist himself and from others." Once the artist achieves this emotional distance from the epical event, the "narrative is no longer purely personal" (*P*, 215).

As Joyce completed *A Portrait of the Artist as a Young Man* he also began a major new phase in his literary career by writing *Exiles* and beginning the writing of *Ulysses.*[1] Though his work remained autobiographical and the personality of the artist never strayed far from center stage, epical event, or dream consciousness, Joyce progressed from his novel of youthful struggle, discovery, and flight to a drama of the artist's return, after a nine-year exile, to face the emotional consequences of "the language of my youth"[2] and to an epic of modern life in which the aspirations and ordeals of the artist are placed within the context of common experience. While his drama of the returning exile proved premature within the context of Joyce's own career, his modern epic developed into one of the most remarkable achievements in modern literature and gave Joyce both the adoration and the notoriety usually accorded the giants of literary history.

Exiles

In his "Notes by the Author" Joyce described *Exiles* as a play of "three cat and mouse acts" (*E*, 123). His critics have in turn offered their own varied interpretations and judgments. Some have praised or criticized *Exiles* as imitation Ibsen, the problem play Joyce was destined to write because of his youthful admiration for the "old master." Others, less concerned with the domestic and social realism of the play, have probed its psychological depths and found archetypes and complexes rather than Ibsen lurking in its depths. Mediating between critical positions, Bernard Benstock first asserts that "with the obvious exception of the poems in *Chamber Music, Exiles* retains the essentials of a nineteenth-century work quite unlike the major literary works of James Joyce" but eventually concludes that *Exiles,* with its unresolved tensions and inner conflicts, also becomes an internalized "drama of 'convalescence,' of wounds that neither heal nor destroy."[3]

While disagreeing on Joyce's level of execution and success in *Exiles,* his critics generally recognize and agree on the play's importance to the Joyce canon because of its advancement of the strong autobiographical elements and key themes in *A Portrait* and its anticipation of Joyce's major concerns in *Ulysses.*[4] To a certain extent *Exiles* projects Stephen Dedalus, the self-declared artist and exile, his confidants and potential betrayers, and his idealized beloved and temptress into the dramatic personae of Richard Rowan, Robert Hand, Beatrice Justice, and Bertha. In the play the potentiality expressed in discourse, dream, and declaration in *A Portrait* is given dramatic actuality in the interlocking emotional triangles played out in the cat-and-mouse movements of the four main characters. The imagined call in *A Portrait* to live, err, and fall has been answered in *Exiles* by the reality of experience as the exile returns to Ireland and undergoes a painful encounter with the consequences of his earlier decision and flight.

In the first act of *Exiles* Joyce demonstrates the personalities and tensions of his drama with four brief but intimate exchanges and revelations between his central characters. The opening scene between Richard Rowan and Beatrice Justice draws out Richard's pride, scorn, and loneliness, even though he has returned to Ireland as a successful writer, as it also reveals Beatrice as the inspiration for Richard's work, even though she describes herself as "convalescent" and Bertha later calls her that "diseased woman" (*E,* 22, 54). Besides unveiling the intellectual and spiritual attraction and bond between Richard and Beatrice the scene also exposes the past bitterness between Richard and his mother and his inability or unwillingness to release himself from his memories of her: "I fought against her spirit while she lived to the bitter end. *He presses his hand to his forehead.* It fights against me still—in here" (*E,* 23). His struggle, obviously reminiscent of Stephen Dedalus's strained relationship with his mother in *A Portrait,* also anticipates Stephen's nightmarish vision of his dead mother in *Ulysses* and his obsession with *amor matris.*

With Richard's character, inner conflict, and vulnerability established, Beatrice fades from the scene and, for the most part, from the rest of the play, as Robert Hand and Bertha step forward to display their attraction for each other and their respective roles as disciple and mistress either desiring or willing to betray Richard's friendship and intimacy. In the scene between Robert and Bertha, Robert boldly confronts Bertha and, after expressing his passion for her, invites her to come to his cottage that evening. With the dramatic conflict of *Exiles* emotionally and physically visible, the remaining scenes in the first act heighten tension while revealing new depths of character and motivation. Robert, his real passion seemingly concealed, declares his faith in Richard as Ireland's intellectual and cultural messiah and his determination to place Richard in a leadership position, first as university chair of romance literature, in the forging of a new Ireland. In return for "the faith of a disciple in his master" (*E,* 44) Robert asks that Richard control his "fierce indignation" and allow Robert to use his position and skills as a journalist to make Richard's past life as exile more palatable: "I understand your pride and your sense of liberty. I understand their point of view also. However, there is a way out; it is simply this. Refrain from contradicting any rumours you may hear concerning what happened . . . or did not happen after you went away. Leave the rest to me" (*E,* 39).

Richard responds to Robert's declaration of faith and intention by claiming knowledge of a faith even stranger than that of the disciple for the master: "the faith of the master in the disciple who will betray him" (*E,* 44). That Robert is willing to betray comes as no surprise after the previous scene's revelation of his darker motivation. In the next scene, however, Richard's apparent intuition reveals itself as an intimate knowledge of Robert's attempted seduction of Bertha. The final revelation in the first act is that Bertha tells Richard everything that has happened and Richard, though he regards Robert as a thief and a fool, is apparently willing to grant Bertha complete liberty to decide whether or not to give herself to Robert. The first act ends with Bertha's decision and Richard's faith as the unresolved dramatic issues, though Richard's inner conflicts have yet to be completely exposed.

The second act shifts to Robert's cottage, as exposition of character and intention gives way to dramatic confrontation and approaching climax. In the first of three scenes Richard arrives at the cottage, thereby revealing to Robert that he knows about his disciple's intended betrayal. After Robert's disconcerting expression of relief at being saved, Richard adds further complexities to his emotional triangle with Robert and Bertha, first by questioning Robert's and, by extension, his own faith in "the luminous certitude that yours is the brain in contact with which she must think and understand and that yours is the body in contact with which her body must feel" (*E,* 63). Admitting he once had this certitude, Richard then questions the emotional consequences of his decision to take Bertha with him into exile, that he may have killed the "virginity of her soul" by taking away "her girlhood, her laughter, her young beauty, the hopes of her young heart" (*E,* 67). Finally Richard confesses his darkest truth to Robert, that despite his noble claim that he does not want Robert to act falsely and secretly against their friendship, "in the very core of my ignoble heart I longed to be betrayed by you and by her—in the dark, in the night—secretly, meanly, craftily. By you my best friend and by her" (*E,* 70).

With Richard's secret doubt, fear, and shame exposed, Robert proposes to Richard not a duel for Bertha but a battle of their souls against the specters of fidelity and friendship. Richard can hardly refuse because Robert phrases his challenge in the proud, defiant language of Richard's youth. In the following scene Richard apparently frees himself from fidelity by releasing Bertha from her bond to him: "Bertha, love him, be his, give yourself to him if you desire—or if you can" (*E,* 75). In the last scene of the second act, Robert in turn frees himself from his friendship with Richard by pressing Bertha to confess her love: "Do you love us both—him and also me? Do you, Bertha? The truth! Tell me. Tell me with your eyes. Or speak!" (*E,* 88).

After the exposition, conflict, and anticipated climax of the first two acts, the third and final act of *Exiles* should provide the play's resolution. In *Exiles,* however, Joyce allows no complete revelation of the truth, even though Robert and Bertha are willing to tell Richard what did or did not happen, and offers no final resolution of the play's inner conflict, despite all the claims to freedom and truthfulness. Bertha and Beatrice do come to some understanding, or at least tolerance, of each other, and Robert, before departing, does write his article of support for Richard and tells him that he failed with Bertha. Yet the certainty of the truth is undermined by Robert's dream that Bertha was his in "that sacred night of love" (*E,* 106) and by the demon voices—"of those who say they love me" (*E,* 109)—telling Richard to despair.

With the certainty or knowledge of the truth now an impossibility in *Exiles,* certitude or faith in the truth becomes in the end the play's problem. Even though Bertha—the least devious and most credible character in the play—assures Richard that she is still his "bride in exile" and pleads with him to come back to her, Richard now suffers from "a deep wound of doubt" in his soul that "can never be healed" (*E*, 112). This permanent wound of doubt in Richard's soul, while marking the end of Joyce's cat-and-mouse play, leaves the future life of Richard and Bertha as uncertain as that of Gabriel and Gretta Conroy in "The Dead" and the direction of Richard's future work as uncertain as that of Stephen Dedalus in *A Portrait*. Yet the doubt that wounds Richard Rowan and has disturbed Joyce readers also anticipates the claims made by Stephen in *Ulysses* that error and doubt are the portals of discovery for a man of genius and that his creative acts, ranging from fatherhood to the forging of a new world, are founded upon "incertitude, upon unlikelihood" (*U*, 170). In this respect the incertitude of *Exiles*, like Stephen's errors in *A Portrait*, is a necessary prelude to the creation of the epic world of *Ulysses*.

Ulysses

Ulysses fulfilled Joyce's ambition to create a great work of art, though the novel's frankness and experimentation also assured Joyce's place as one of the most controversial writers of the twentieth century. Out of the unlikelihood of a planned-but-never-written story for *Dubliners* about a cuckolded Dublin Jew, Joyce forged a literary masterpiece so innovative and comprehensive that T. S. Eliot declared *Ulysses*, if a novel at all, the novel to end all novels because it rendered obsolete all previous forms of the novel and closed out all possibilities for the future.[5] Even Virginia Woolf and William Butler Yeats, who judged Joyce's writing as underbred and vulgar, recognized the importance of *Ulysses*, while praising the book's exactitude, intensity, and boldness.[6]

For all its claims to originality, however, *Ulysses* actually extends and embellishes several themes and strategies of Joyce's earlier works and even reprises characters from *Dubliners* and *A Portrait*. At its most realistic level the novel answers the challenge that the newspaper editor Myles Crawford directs at Stephen Dedalus in the "Aeolus" episode: "Give them something with a bite in it. Put us all into it, damn its soul. Father, Son and Holy Ghost and Jakes M'Carthy" (*U*, 111). With the same "scrupulous meanness" of *Dubliners*, Joyce creates in *Ulysses* a complete day in the life of Dublin, beginning with the morning hours of 16 June 1904, now celebrated in the literary world as Bloomsday, and ending in the early hours of the following day. The collection of characters that make up the composite landscape of *Dubliners* now become, with numerous additions, the "Jakes M'Carthys" or supporting cast of *Ulysses* and in the process give the book, as Richard Kain points out, its "considerable verisimilitude" while adding a robustness and humor not found in *Dubliners* and *A Portrait.*[7]

Joyce also extends the literary life of Stephen Dedalus into *Ulysses,* but, with the artist no longer the center of emotional gravity and the narrative no longer purely personal, Stephen's impressions and conflicts play a greatly reduced role in determining the narrative style and structure of *Ulysses.* Still the young man of *A Portrait* rather than the older artist of *Exiles,* Stephen, after only a brief exile in Paris, has been called back to Dublin by his father's telegram telling Stephen of his mother's dying. Now troubled by memories of her death but unshaken in his conviction of his own genius and mission, Stephen wanders through the hours of *Ulysses* haunted by his nightmarish dream of his mother's "wasted body within its loose grave clothes" (*U,* 9) but still seeking an understanding of the way in which the artist transforms life's experiences into radiant beauty. Moving in and out of rather than directing the narrative flow of *Ulysses,* Stephen encounters the same nets of his childhood and the same companions willing to betray. Yet while developing another aesthetic theory and declaring once again that he will not serve that which threatens his freedom, he meets and shares a brief period with a character who appears to have the potential for affecting and even influencing his perceptions.

Frank Budgen maintains that with the invention of Leopold Bloom Joyce moved from the limited, pictorial art of self-portraiture to an expansive, plastic art of infinite contours and angles. In Stephen and Bloom, Budgen states, "There is a difference of dimension and substance as well as of character. Stephen is self-portrait, and therefore one-sided. Bloom is seen from all angles, as no self-portrait can be seen. He is as plastic as Stephen is pictorial."[8] The disadvantage of the self-portrait is that the artist not only writes about himself but also models for himself. As writer of and model for himself the artist is limited to a choice between two dimensions, in Joyce's case in *A Portrait* between the heroic and the ironic. When the artist, according to Budgen, selects any object other than himself, he has "the whole compass to choose from. He can walk around any other model but not round himself" (Budgen, 62).

For many readers of *Ulysses* Leopold Bloom is that well-rounded character, and for some he is the most completely and intimately drawn figure in the history of literature. In direct contrast to the artistic-sided Stephen, Bloom is perceived variously as a Dublin Odysseus, a modern Everyman, a compassionate humanist, an existential hero, and even, as Ezra Pound declared, "a great man" (Letters, 2:423). A 38-year-old Dublin Jew, Bloom after the first three chapters or Telemachiad becomes the major narrative presence in Ulysses. As he struggles with his own memories, including those associated with the deaths of his father and his son, he goes about the ordinary processes of living and the business of making his living as a canvasser for advertisements. He also, however, encounters some extraordinary, or at least not-so-ordinary, situations and characters during his Dublin odyssey while undergoing the painful ordeal of knowing, even to the hour of the day, that his wife will turn him into a cuckold.

Though Molly Bloom, the third major figure in Joyce's equidistant configuration of characters in Ulysses, does not have the narrative presence of Stephen and Bloom until the celebrated final chapter of Ulysses, she has inspired the same critical raves and rages as her male counterparts. She has been praised by her admirers as a mother-earth figure, a modern-day Penelope, patient and faithful in her fashion, while her interior monologue has been described by Jung as "a string of veritable psychological peaches" (Letters, 3:253). Her detractors, however, see her as promiscuous, vulgar, and ignorant and her monologue as a concoction of male fantasies and fears rather than a marvel of insight, as Jung claims, into "the real psychology of a woman" (Letters, 3:253). Molly Bloom has the final word in Ulysses, but readers disagree on the signification of her "yes" to Joyce's comic vision in Ulysses.[9]

While Joyce's critics, in making their own odyssey through Ulysses, have perceived symbolic depths and cosmic meaning and purpose underlying the verisimilitude of character and event, the invitation for their search, though not necessarily the responsibility for their claims, has come directly from the narrative strategies of the novel itself. The call to adventure or perhaps the siren's call to the reader of Ulysses draws attention to the novel's stream of consciousness, a refinement of the impressionism of A Portrait; its elaborate mythical structure, emerging out of echoes of Joyce's earlier works; and its stylistic embellishments and complexities, which appear to take on a life of their own, beginning with the intrusive and curious newspaper headlines in the "Aeolus" episode.

Joyce's experimental advancement—from an impressionistic narrative limited in its range of language and form to the perceptions and personality of the central character to a stream of consciousness that further records the thoughts of the controlling character—appears, at least as a glimmer, on the first page of *Ulysses* when the word *Chrysostomos* interposes itself in an early passage describing the actions of Buck Mulligan: "He peered sideways up and gave a long slow whistle of call, then paused awhile in rapt attention, his even white teeth glistening here and there with gold points. Chrysostomos. Two strong shrill whistles answered through the calm" (*U, 3*). A few pages later interposition becomes intervention with a narrative flair when Mulligan waves a mirror in front of Stephen and invites him to have one good look at himself: "Stephen bent forward and peered at the mirror held out to him, cleft by a crooked crack. Hair on end. As he and others see me. Who chose this face for me? This dogsbody to rid of vermin. It asks me too" (*U, 6*).

The shift in narrative midstream, once Stephen looks into the cracked looking glass, from the third person to the first person signals a brief movement inward, as do the fragmented sentences, to Stephen's conscious thoughts and invites the reader by retrospection to see "Chrysostomos" as Stephen's conscious but unspoken reaction to Mulligan's annoying rhetoric and gold fillings, because the word refers to a church founder famous for his golden-mouthed rhetoric. This movement between externally recorded impressions and internally measured thought, sometimes termed an indirect interior monologue, becomes the main narrative pattern in *Ulysses* until the last chapter, when the stream of Molly Bloom flows, without interruption or intrusion from an external voice, into a direct interior monologue. Even when the elaborate style in the later chapters of *Ulysses* appears to undermine and eventually usurp the narrative, the stream of impressions and thoughts still provide what Joyce, according to Stuart Gilbert, called "a bridge over which to march his eighteen episodes."[10]

As Joyce expanded character and experimented with narration he also introduced an elaborate mythical structure to *Ulysses* based upon Homer's *Odyssey*. Beginning with the title of his novel he used the *Odyssey* to create Homeric echoes and correspondences, especially with characters, settings, episodes, and narrative structure.[11] Stephen Dedalus, Leopold Bloom, and Molly Bloom have their mythical counterparts in Telemachus, Odysseus, and Penelope, just as minor characters like Mr. Deasy, the Citizen, and Bella Cohen bear likeness to Nestor, the Cyclops, and Circe. *Ulysses* also follows the three-part Homeric structure with its first three chapters, or *Telemachiad,* following the early movements of Stephen; its main body of twelve chapters devoted for the most part to Leopold Bloom's adventures; and its last three chapters, or *Nostos,* following Bloom's return home with Stephen. The eighteen chapters, or episodes, of *Ulysses* are, with the exception of "Wandering Rocks," gleaned from the twenty-four books of the *Odyssey* and take their now-commonly-used titles (which do not appear in the text of *Ulysses*) from an elaborate schema Joyce devised to help friends in their reading and understanding of the novel. Though Joyce insisted on absolute secrecy from his friends and refused to allow Bennett Cerf to publish the schema in Random House's American edition of *Ulysses,* various schemata have been published, including the most familiar version in Stuart Gilbert's *James Joyce's "Ulysses,"* a book encouraged and directed by Joyce himself.

Some critics believe that Gilbert's book on Homeric parallels has been both Pandora's box and cornucopia in generating a flood of mythical and symbolic studies of *Ulysses.* Bernard Benstock, however, observes a more diffused critical response: the "centrality of Homer's text to that of James Joyce has been stressed by some readers, the parody of a heroic epic in a novel of the mundane world by other readers, and the mere casualness of associations by still others" (Benstock, 98). A. Walton Litz suggests that readers of *Ulysses* have generally assumed critical positions first claimed by Ezra Pound and T. S. Eliot.[12] While praising *Ulysses* for its unity of style and uncompromising realism, Pound dismissed the Homeric parallels as little more than a scaffold. For Pound *Ulysses* was "the realistic novel par excellence."[13] Eliot, however, saw Joyce moving beyond Flaubert and James by using myth not as embellishment but as "a way of controlling, of ordering, of giving a shape and a significance to the immense panorama of futility and anarchy which is contemporary history."[14]

Admiring *Ulysses* for either its Flaubertian realism or its mythical method, Pound and Eliot preferred to pass over or merely acknowledge the stylistic innovations of the later chapters. During the composition of *Ulysses* Pound suggested that Joyce consider bringing Stephen Dedalus forward again and complained that "a new style per chapter not required" (Ellmann, 459). Karen Lawrence contends that "until well into the 1970s, most book-length studies of *Ulysses* paid little attention to its radical stylistic changes"; in trying to come to terms with narrative complexities and disruptions Joyce "critics and teachers tended to focus on character, symbol, and myth rather than style."[15]

The critical approaches to the style of *Ulysses* begin with early attempts to work through the novel's later embellishments, elaborations, and experiments by not straying far from Joyce's narrative bridge or by drawing narrative threads out of mythical and symbolic patterns. Other approaches, including more recent studies, prefer to see the stylistic changes not as problems to overcome but as symptomatic of the most radical development in *Ulysses*. Rather than the style of *Ulysses* serving the novel's narrative, it begins, with the "Aeolus" headlines, to assert its own identity as arranger, performer, and eventually consciousness of the book itself.[16] From this perspective *Ulysses* begins as an experimental novel, but instead of progressing toward meaning and resolution the book in midstream develops into a self-reflexive text that explores its own possibilities of language and style while undermining the narrative authority of its earlier chapters.[17]

Another possible approach to the style of *Ulysses* is to see the radical changes not as Joyce's abandonment of Aristotelian actualities but as his further recognition of external reality and its influence on his characters' hourly movements and thoughts. In *A Portrait* Joyce developed his impressionistic narrative of Stephen's childhood, adolescence, and young manhood within the ineluctable movement of the seasons and the irresistible rhythm of the body and soul. In *Ulysses* Joyce, limiting his novel to the span of a day rather than a young lifetime, measured his epic of modern life, with its precise realism, narrative flow, mythical parallels, and stylistic permutations, to the dance of the hours.

In the "Calypso" episode Leopold Bloom remembers the morning "after the bazaar dance when May's band played Ponchielli's dance of the hours. Explain that: morning hours, noon, then evening coming on, then night hours" (*U,* 57). After revealing the reason his mind has returned to the bazaar dance—that it was the occasion of his wife's first attraction to Blazes Boylan—Bloom further recalls the performance of the dance of the hours: "Evening hours, girls in grey gauze. Night hours then: black with daggers and eyemasks. Poetical idea: pink, then golden, then grey, then black. Still, true to life also. Day: then the night" (*U,* 57). Hours later, in the "Circe" episode, Bloom's memory becomes phantasm as the Hours, appropriately clad and sequentially arranged, join in the whirling dance at the brothel until they are dismissed by Stephen's phantasm, prompted by his perception of the dance of the hours as a veiled "Dance of death" (*U,* 472) of the emaciated corpse of his mother, risen from the grave to challenge Stephen's rebellious pride.

Stuart Gilbert maintains that the dance of the hours, important thematically to *Ulysses*, also "suggests symbolically the time-structure of the entire book" (Gilbert, 140). The dance of the hours may also, however, suggest a reason or justification for the stylistic maneuverings in *Ulysses*. Instead of undermining the book's verisimilitude the changes in style, as complex and challenging as they are to the reader, may simply be a reminder of the ineluctable modality of the physical world to human consciousness. Just as Ponchielli's musical score modulates and the performers' costumes vary in recognition of the mutability of the hours, so does the style of *Ulysses*, after the steady, unobtrusive circulation of the morning hours, react, even if mockingly, to the hourly activities that give shape and substance to the day. Beginning with the noon hour in *Ulysses* the activities of the day, as the physical or public world of Dublin becomes more visible and audible, influence the book's language and narrative as much as the thoughts and perceptions of Joyce's characters. As Stephen and Leopold Bloom circulate through the streets of Dublin on a narrative odyssey that will end at 7 Eccles Street with Molly Bloom's interior monologue, their hourly encounters with the life of Dublin modulate and color events and preoccupations, social and individual, with a rhetoric ranging from the blaring headlines of "Aeolus" to the impersonal catechism of "Ithaca." These radical stylistic changes may signal Joyce's forsaking of the narrative realities of the early chapters in *Ulysses* for the playful possibilities of the style itself, but they may also reflect Joyce's vision of the relationship between the word and the world as collaboration rather than usurpation.

The odyssey of Joyce's *Ulysses*, with its labyrinth of narrative, structure, and style, begins with the three-episode *Telemachiad* that reintroduces the character of Stephen Dedalus and, as C. H. Peake observes, also takes up or recalls many of the themes and supporting characters of *A Portrait:* "*Ulysses* opens, like a sequel, on 16 June 1904. In the interval, Stephen has escaped from Dublin to Paris, having flown above the nets intended to trap him, but, now that he is back in *Dublin,* the closing triumph of the *Portrait* is seen to have been illusory."[18] In "Telemachus" Joyce places Stephen at the waking hour of 8:00 A.M. in a Martello tower that he shares with Buck Mulligan, a medical student, and a guest, the Englishman Haines. As Mulligan prepares to shave he mockingly intones the Introit of the Mass, much to Stephen's irritation, and thereby sets the tone for the entire hour. During the episode Joyce, while establishing his basic narrative strategy, or bridge, as an interplay between conscious perception and thought, has Mulligan ridicule as absurd that which has held value for Stephen, from his family name—"The mockery of it!" (*U*, 3)—and his artistic posturing—"If Wilde were only alive to see you" (*U*, 6)—to his aesthetic theorizing—"I'm not equal to Thomas Aquinas and the fifty five reasons he has made to prop it up. Wait till I have a few pints in me first" (*U*, 15).

The narrative interplay between Stephen and Mulligan also reveals that the news of his mother's dying has brought Stephen back to Dublin and that the memories of his mother's death have since haunted him and undermined his resolve: "Her glazing eyes, staring out of death, to shake and bend my soul" (*U*, 9). The revelation of Stephen's remorse over his mother's death is, however, merely the emotional fulcrum in a narrative that makes vivid the dangers to his artistic mission. When in his conversation with Haines Stephen claims he is the servant of two masters, the Catholic Church and the British Empire, and then adds a third, the Ireland that wants him for "odd jobs," he is merely formulating his resentment of Haines's intrusion, his distress over his own refusal to kneel at his mother's deathbed, and his embarrassment at the fawning ignorance of the milkwoman, whom Stephen has imaged as the "poor old woman" (*U*, 12) or as a symbol of Ireland itself. As the episode closes Stephen has confirmed that he is still threatened by the nets of religion and politics, still alienated from family and friends—"I will not sleep here tonight. Home also I cannot go" (*U*, 19)—and believes more than ever that those who claim his love or friendship are only too willing to betray his true nature and purpose as the artist. Stephen's last thought and word in the episode is also his judgment of Mulligan's real intent—"Usurper" (*U*, 19).

After the revelations of "Telemachus," the narrative turns in "Nestor" and "Proteus" to expose even further Stephen's vulnerability to both his actual world and his private thoughts. The "Nestor" episode finds Stephen at the 10:00 A.M. hour going through the motions of teaching school. Now appearing more frequently and intrusively in the narrative, his thoughts, reflecting the history lesson being taught on Pyrrhus, brood on the reality of historical events: "They are not to be thought away. Time has branded them and fettered they are lodged in the room of the infinite possibilities they have ousted" (*U*, 21). Stephen's dilemma is that he apprehends the applicability to history of Aristotle's definition of movement as "an actuality of the possible as possible" (*U*, 21), but he also realizes, as he informs Mr. Deasy, that history "is a nightmare from which I am trying to awake" (*U*, 28).

While Aristotle's "slender sentences" (*P*, 176) offer the reader another thread connecting the narratives of *A Portrait* and *Ulysses* and give the Stephen of *Ulysses* the intellectual perspective and definitions he will need in "Proteus" and "Scylla and Charybdis," his Aristotelian definition of history strongly suggests he is mistaken in thinking he will ever completely escape the nightmare of Irish history or his own life: "What if that nightmare gave you a back kick?" (*U, 28*). Rejecting Mr. Deasy's Newtonian definition of history as the movement "towards one great goal, the manifestation of God" (*U, 28*), Stephen nevertheless spends his time in "Nestor" teaching history, contemplating the relics of the past, and breaking a lance with an old man whose pro-British, anti-Semitic, misogynistic attitudes represent the worse manifestations of human history. Preferring the chaos of youth to the tyrannical imposition of the past, Stephen dismisses Mr. Deasy as an ancient betrayer—"On his wise shoulders through the checkerwork of leaves the sun flung spangles, dancing coins" (*U, 30*)—but, as Stephen turns his back on history as he has already walked away from friendship even he knows that he still has much to learn and overcome before forging a permanent image out of the chaos of his own life.

In "Proteus" Stephen, now left to his own thoughts, walks at the 11:00 A.M. hour along Sandymount strand. As he contemplates the irresistible manifestations of space and time to the perceiving mind, the narrative, though not completely submerged in thought as it is in "Penelope," expresses itself more compellingly in the language of Stephen's consciousness than it has in previous episodes. Striding closer and closer to the incoming tides, Stephen first experiments with his own sensory perception of the visible by closing his eyes, only to discover that reality merely asserts itself to his auditory sense. When he opens his eyes he proves with his own sight the ineluctable character of the physical world—"There all the time without you: and ever shall be, world without end" (*U, 31*)—just as by closing his eyes he has validated Aristotle's dictum that the object perceived is not present in the perceived image.

Having surrendered the tower key to the usurper Mulligan and the classroom to the bigot Deasy, Stephen now tries to bring some meaning and order—with the help of the speculations of the great and rebellious intellects of philosophy and religion—to the protean relationship between his own consciousness and the visible universe. As, however, he struggles intellectually with the real nature of relationships, ranging from the act of apperception to the consubstantiality of Father and Son, Stephen in his mind's eye creates impressive images out of his personal and racial heritage that confirm his potential as artist, even as his relationships with family, friends, and history threaten to drown that potential. Although Stephen, who stops short of the sea's great flow, cannot overcome the turmoil of his own mind, he imagines a visit to his Aunt Sara's out of the flux of family memories, re-creates a conversation with the exiled Kevin Egan out of his own brief exile in Paris, images a scene and a dramatis persona for himself out of ancient Irish history, and reshapes human distractions into midwives and gypsies and sea wrack into literary signatures. While his visible movements and literary efforts in "Proteus" are either gross or ineffectual, Stephen leaves behind a rich display of imaginings that shows his genius for self-mockery, for re-creating history, and for someday forging his art out of the protean flux of human and racial consciousness: "He turned his face over a shoulder, rere regardant. Moving through the air high spars of a threemaster, her sails brailed up on the crosstrees, homing, upstream, silently moving, a silent ship" (*U,* 42).

Just as the closing image of the *Telemachiad* anticipates the appearance of Ulyssean Leopold Bloom in the "Calypso" episode, the narrative of "Calypso" by returning to the morning hours appears to herald Bloom's appearance as the real beginning of the novel. With Stephen, who sees himself as pretender, finally deposed, the narrative can properly begin its odyssey of everyday life. Another possibility, however, is that the narrative returns to the 8:00 A.M. hour to confirm not only the ineluctable modality of the visible but also its separate reality from human consciousness. As the young artist awakens to a sea of troubles, the ordinary citizen, there all the time without Stephen, also prepares himself for his own daily adventures and ordeals. Beginning with "Calypso" the narrative further confirms the separate identities and natures of Stephen and Bloom as they move through common locations and events, even resting at the same moments and places, only to move off to separate destinations and destinies by narrative's end.

Unlike Stephen, who wanders off into uncertainty, Leopold Bloom begins and ends his journey at 7 Eccles Street. The narrative locates Bloom preparing breakfast in bed for his wife, Molly, as he contemplates satisfying his own morning appetite with the inner organ of beast or fowl. In "Calypso" Bloom goes about his morning business, purchasing a pork kidney, serving breakfast to Molly, reading the morning mail, eating his own breakfast, and finally relieving his bowels, as the narrative, reinforcing and extending Joyce's bridge, records the interplay between Bloom's perceptions and his conscious thoughts. For the next three episodes, however, the narrative becomes less abstract, allusive, and self-absorbed and more concrete, practical, and responsive to external realities as Bloom replaces Stephen as central consciousness.

Much of the narrative of "Calypso" offers a rhetorical display of Bloom's practical curiosity and impressionable mind. He speculates on a wide range of subjects, from the behavior of the family cat to Ponchielli's dance of the hours, as his moods and interests shift according to the impression or urging of the moment. A passing cloud covering the sun can change his perspective and mood—"No, not like that. A barren land, bare waste" (*U, 50*)—as easily as the movement of his bowels can prompt thoughts on the best fertilizers. The episode, however, also provides the reader with fragments of information about Bloom's family history—"She knew from the first poor little Rudy wouldn't live" (*U, 54*)—and his present crisis—"O, Boylan, she said. He's bringing the programme" (*U, 52*)—that will form important patterns during Bloom's day. Even his speculations on metempsychosis— "That we all lived before on the earth thousands of years ago" (*U, 53*)—alert the reader to the mythical possibilities of the book as Bloom prepares to leave the allurements of "Calypso" and begin his odyssey through the streets of Dublin.

In "Lotus-Eaters" Bloom, at the hour Stephen Dedalus is teaching school, drifts about Dublin preparatory to attending the funeral of "Poor Dignam" (*U, 57*). Bloom fills the hour by visiting the post office, where he picks up a letter addressed to his pseudonym, Henry Flower. He also sits in on the conclusion of morning Mass at All Hallow's Church, stops at the chemist's to fill a lotion prescription for his wife, and while there purchases a cake of soap for a morning bath, which he anticipates taking as the episode comes to an end. As Bloom moves about, his mind once again fills the narrative with speculations, mostly on the attraction of opiates, and private revelations, including a reading of the letter from Martha Clifford and an allusion to his father's suicide: "Perhaps he was a woman. Why Ophelia committed suicide. Poor papa" (*U, 62*). Bloom's physical and mental wanderings, however, are also disrupted by a chance meeting with McCoy that allows for more information on Molly Bloom's singing career and by a moment of miscommunication with Bantam Lyons that will have disastrous consequences for Bloom. As Bloom cheerfully contemplates the pleasure of his bath Bantam Lyons is speeding off with the mistaken notion that Bloom's stated intention of throwing away his newspaper was actually a tip to bet on Throwaway, a dark horse entered in the Ascot Gold Cup race. Hours later, in "Cyclops," Bloom will pay dearly for Lyon's misreading.

Bloom's first public ordeal, however, comes about in the claustro-phobic conditions and atmosphere of the "Hades" episode. As he rides in the funeral carriage with Jack Power, Martin Cunningham, and Simon Dedalus, Bloom suffers through several painful embarrassments and humiliations, some coincidental and unintentional but others clearly pointed at Bloom. Simon Dedalus's outburst against Buck Mulli-gan, provoked by Bloom's sighting of Stephen as the carriage passes through Sandymount, prompts Bloom to remember and regret the death of his own son: "If little Rudy had lived. See him grow up. Hear his voice in the house. Walking beside Molly in an Eton suit. My son" (*U,* 73). A few minutes later, when Martin Cunningham spots Blazes Boylan, Bloom hides his anxiety by staring at his nails, but he also has to endure the humiliation of answering questions about Molly's concert tour. After the two coincidences Bloom sits through the further discom-fort of listening to a racially pointed story about the moneylender Ruben J. Dodd and his son that is followed by Power's condemnation of suicide: "The greatest disgrace to have in the family" (*U,* 79). Even at the cemetery Bloom, after his curt treatment in the carriage, endures yet another embarrassment when he is slighted by John Henry Menton.

Bloom's humiliating experiences in "Hades" and his own painful thoughts of his son's death, his wife's likely infidelity, and his father's suicide place him in a state of emotional turmoil coincidental and parallel to Stephen's intellectual struggle in "Proteus." Whereas Ste-phen contends against the protean flux of his own consciousness, Bloom must overcome the depressing state of his own emotions, especially as he strolls about the cemetery grounds and sees a huge rat wriggling itself under a stone crypt. Just as Stephen's artistic character and poten-tial momentarily rescue him from his own thoughts, Bloom's resilient and instinctive nature overcomes his surroundings and his own dismal mood: "Back to the world again. Enough of this place. . . . Plenty to see and hear and feel yet. Feel live warm beings near you. Let them sleep in their maggoty beds. They not going to get me this innings. Warm beds: warm fullblooded life" (*U,* 94).

Bloom's own nature assures his passage through the Dublin under-world, but the narrative of "Hades" marks its own path of return to the noon world of "Aeolus." While the appearance or mention of so many ghosts from *Dubliners* appears to reinforce the bleak hopelessness of the hour, the numerous mythical echoes from Odysseus's trip to the under-world act as a comic counterpoise to what Stuart Gilbert describes as the episode's "mortuary atmosphere" (Gilbert, 173). In other words the narrative's own resiliency in drawing mythical counterparts—Martin Cunningham and Sisyphus, Paddy Dignam and Elpenor, Father Coffey and Cerberus, John O'Connell and Hades—restores an equilibrium in *Ulysses,* similar to the effect of Stephen's self-mockery in "Proteus," between the mean-spirited world of Dublin and the irrepressible manifestations of the human comedy, while further affirming the infinite possibilities of language, style, and vision in the juxtaposition of the ironic and the heroic.

In "Aeolus" the narrative draws even more attention to itself with its intrusive headlines and whirlwind of rhetorical devices. Joyce's narrative bridge, already shaken by two incidents in "Hades" where characters appear to speak beyond the range of Bloom's hearing, actually disappears, at least briefly, when Bloom leaves the newspaper office moments before Stephen arrives. Yet the narrative disruptions and uncertainties, while diverting attention from the movement of character, event, and thought, also serve to undermine the claims of the Dublin crowd on the art of rhetoric. As Peake observes, for all the effusive rhetoric in and about the chapter Joyce's strategy actually contrasts "the true rhetorical tradition of Ireland, represented by men of an earlier generation like Taylor and Bushe, with the debased forms displayed by the editor and his cronies" (Peake, 194). This strategy, then, underscores the jeopardy for Bloom and Stephen in the inflated, debased rhetoric of the day. Bloom endures even more indignities as he navigates through the verbal rebuffs in his effort to secure an advertisement for the House of Keyes. Stephen, on the other hand, encounters more alluring winds as the editor invites him to write something for the paper. Though Bloom and Stephen barely miss each other in "Aeolus," the narrative ends with Bloom left behind in the rhetorical wake of Myles Crawford's insults, while Stephen, offering up his "Parable of the Plums," becomes the moving spirit as the press-gang sails off for a round of drinks.

After the pyrotechnics of "Aeolus" Joyce's narrative, remaining behind with Bloom, returns, in "Lestrygonians," to the familiar strategies of the first six chapters. The hour, advancing toward 2:00 P.M., is in Bloom's mind "the very worse time of day. Vitality. Dull, gloomy: hate this hour. Feel as if I had been eaten and spewed" (*U,* 135). For outcast Bloom his preoccupation during the hour is with his appetite. Once again he wanders about Dublin, this time considering a place to eat, as his thoughts and, accordingly, the style of the episode are basted with food imagery. When Bloom enters the Burton, however, the narrative intention of "Lestrygonians" clearly reveals itself as more than stylistic virtuousity: "Stink gripped his trembling breath: pungent meatjuice, slush of greens. See the animals feed. . . . Spaton sawdust, sweetish warmish cigarettesmoke, reek of plug, spilt beer, men's beery piss, the stale of ferment. . . . Couldn't eat a morsel here" (*U*, 138–39). His decision to eat a light meal at Davy Byrne's "Moral pub" (*U*, 140), his temperate response to his own hunger, and his disgust with the gluttony of his fellow Dubliners reveal Bloom's natural virtue even though his narrative presence continues to attract suspicion, rudeness, and at times barely concealed contempt and hostility. Hardly to the midpoint of his travels Bloom has already illustrated the prudence and temperance of the "good man," though impending hours and trials will also test his fortitude and sense of justice before he returns to his warm bed.

At the end of "Lestrygonians" Bloom, after helping a blind stripling across the street, spots Boylan once again and barely escapes an embarrassing encounter by heading for the National Museum. In the next episode, at the National Library, the narrative control shifts back to Stephen Dedalus's consciousness but not to the previous hour, as Stephen, after his rounds of drinks, prepares to offer his theory of Shakespeare to a doubting audience of Dublin literary figures, including George Russell, John Eglinton, Richard Best, T. W. Lyster, and the late-arriving antagonist, Buck Mulligan.

Though Stephen has struggled with his private thoughts since the opening of the novel, he faces his most severe public trial in "Scylla and Charybdis." Opposed by Neoplatonic views of literature that range from Russell's belief in spiritual essences to Best's "tame essence of Wilde" (*U*, 163), not invited to George Moore's gathering of young artists, mocked by Mulligan's barbs and his own thoughts, Aristotelian Stephen composes a theory of artistic creation out of the body of Shakespeare's work and life. As his mind plays with literary language, rhythm, and forms Stephen uses *Hamlet,* the most personal and universal of Shakespeare's plays, as the touchstone for an elaborate ghost story of betrayal and banishment heralded by the appearance of Shakespeare in the role of the king: "Is it possible that player Shakespeare, a ghost by absence, and in the vesture of buried Denmark, a ghost by death, speaking his own words to his own son's name (had Hamnet Shakespeare lived he would have been prince Hamlet's twin), is it possible, I want to know, or probable that he did not draw or foresee the logical conclusion of those premises: you are the dispossessed son: I am the murdered father: your mother is the guilty queen, Ann Shakespeare, born Hathaway?" (*U*, 155). Stephen's portrait of Shakespeare, based on his crafty arrangement of "those premises," begins with the older woman Ann Hathaway seducing young Shakespeare, thereby dispossessing him of his youth and self-confidence: "Belief in himself has been untimely killed" (*U*, 161). Banished from life's feast, Stephen's Shakespeare later endures the corruption of his name and heritage when Ann commits adultery with Shakespeare's brothers, Edmund and Richard, who now share their given name with Shakespeare's greatest villains. According to Stephen, Shakespeare, denied his manhood and usurped of any real claims to title and respect, actually forged his dramatic art out of his incertitude and unlikelihood, thereby creating in the actual world of his dramatic art images of that which remained unexperienced and unfulfilled in his own life. The journey through Shakespeare's play, then, becomes inevitably a return to the artist himself: "Every life is many days, day after day. We walk through ourselves, meeting robbers, ghosts, giants, old men, young men, wives, widows, brothers-in-love, but always meeting ourselves" (*U*, 175).

When asked if he believes his own theory Stephen says no, but whether or not he believes in the Shakespeare he has invented his theory has obvious relevance to his own private turmoil and present trial. Stephen's struggle with his remorse and fear, projected into the ghoulish image of his dead mother, now finds literary expression in the emotional wound suffered by Shakespeare in his youth. His resentment of those who have mocked him and usurped his place as artist expresses itself in the image of the traitorous brothers. *Hamlet*, Shakespeare's revenge play, points the way, then, for Stephen to overcome his problems and his enemies. Faced with betrayal and banishment, he appears willing to accept his lot: "They mock to try you. Act. Be acted on" (*U*, 173). But he also foresees the time when through his own art he will liberate himself from all forms of entrapment and servitude and avenge himself by trapping the treacherous behavior of Mulligan and the others in the pages of his art, thereby damning their souls forever: "See this. Remember" (*U*, 158).[19]

While Joyce critics continue the debate on whether to believe or disbelieve Stephen's theory, the narrative bridge leads Stephen out of the library and, after another near encounter with Bloom, into the labyrinth of Dublin streets, where Stephen and Bloom become merely parts of the "Wandering Rocks" episode. Some critics, taking their lead from a dotted line Joyce drew between "Scylla and Charybdis" and "Wandering Rocks" on a list of episodes sent to John Quinn, have extended Joyce's act by contending that, beginning with "Wandering Rocks," the narrative bridge breaks down and invention, arrangement, and style dominate the second half of the novel and claim the reader's attention.[20] In his letter to Quinn, however, Joyce wrote that the "dotted line represents the first half, but not part or division—that is, 9 episodes of the 18" (*Letters*, 1:145). In other words Joyce appears to be pointing out a simple mathematical equation rather than claiming a new departure or direction.

"Wandering Rocks" certainly appears as a structural departure, but the episode, praised as both a temporal and spatial tour de force,[21] also extends the earlier episodes' narrative content and strategies to the simultaneous movements and conscious states of other characters, thereby illustrating Stephen's thought—"Throb always without you and the throb always within" (*U*, 199)—and further reinforcing the narrative's collaboration between the word within and the world without. In the episodes within "Wandering Rocks" the narrative brings to life that other world of Stephen and Bloom—the poverty of the Dedalus family, the sexual arrogance of Blazes Boylan—as well as a wide range of the petty concerns, intrigues, frustrations, and accomplishments of Joyce's Dubliners. While the narrative bridge acts as common thoroughfare, the brief moments with Stephen and Bloom, however, are hardly petty to the narrative interests of *Ulysses*. Stephen's book-cart encounter with his sister Dilly is a poignant reminder of his misery in the face of his family's poverty and his fear of drowning in the family's misfortune: "She is drowning. Agenbite. Save her. Agenbite. All against us. She will drown me with her, eyes and hair. Lank coils of seaweed hair around me, my heart, my soul. Salt green death. . . . Misery! Misery!" (*U*, 200). Bloom's narrative moment at the bookshop and his purchase of *Sweets of Sin* for his wife painfully confirm his dilemma and act as prelude to Bloom's private anguish in "Sirens" and his public ordeal in "Cyclops."

"Sirens" has been especially intriguing and frustrating for Joyce critics, whose disagreements on its musical composition have ranged from the fragmented opening, variously described as overture, prelude, or orchestra tuning, to its form and intention—whether Joyce's playfulness reveals the rich musical possibilities of language or the impossibility of language aspiring to the forms and effect of music.[22] Little doubt, however, exists about Joyce's virtuousity in orchestrating the episode, which contains, according to Zack Bowen, "158 references to forty-seven different works of music," though five works, ranging from love songs to patriotic ballads, dominate the narrative (Bowen, 491–92). For all its musical strategies and allusions, "Sirens," following the freewheeling "Wandering Rocks," eventually returns to Bloom's consciousness, one of the novel's main narrative spans, appropriately at the hour of Blazes Boylan's planned visit to 7 Eccles Street—"At four. Near now" (U, 217). Bloom, after a third coincidental sighting, follows Boylan into the Ormond, though his prudence and temperance carry him, with Richie Goulding, into the dining area, where he can discreetly observe Boylan. When Boylan leaves for his adulterous appointment Bloom is left to his dinner and his depression, as the music of the hour variously soothes, distracts, or reminds Bloom of his past and present situations: "Question of mood you're in" (U, 229). After finishing his dinner and writing a note to Martha Clifford, Bloom, bored with the musical diversion, leaves the Ormond and closes an episode filled with verbal notes, including several from earlier episodes, with his own flatulent signature.

"Sirens," perhaps as prelude to the mock-heroic dimensions of "Cyclops," contains several striking mythical echoes and parallels as Joyce's Dubliners are lured by various siren calls to the Ormond. "Sirens" also sets up "Cyclops," at least in Joyce's odyssey, as an emotional sequel, as Bloom now faces his worst public trial of the day. Arriving at Barney Kiernan's for a previously arranged meeting with Cunningham and Power to help with the insurance on the Dignam mortgage, Bloom in "Cyclops" encounters rudeness and hostility far worse than what he has already endured in "Hades" and "Aeolus." Bloom's principal antagonist, the xenophobic Citizen, questions Bloom's claims to nationality, ridicules his character and racial heritage, and, when he mistakingly believes Bloom has won money on the Gold Cup race and refuses to buy a round of drinks, throws a biscuit tin in the direction of the departing Bloom. Usually prudent and temperate, Bloom finally shows fortitude and a sense of justice, at an hour dominated by mean-spiritedness, when he defends himself as an Irish citizen, rejects national hatred, and speaks out against the persecution of his race: "And I belong to a race too, says Bloom, that is hated and persecuted. Also now. This very moment. This very instant" (U, 273).

As Bloom finally reveals himself as Joyce's good man, the narrative of "Cyclops" deserts Bloom and turns for its narrative presence to one of his adversaries, a contemptuous and contemptible bar leech and collector of bad debts. The narrative further distances itself from Bloom's attempted heroics by adding numerous mock-heroic interpolations, which while hilarious appear to undermine the seriousness of Bloom's situation. Though some critics see the disruptive narrative of "Cyclops" as further evidence of Joyce's own desertion of his earlier narrative interests and strategies, the distortions and exaggerations in "Cyclops" are also manifestations of the one-sided or one-eyed perspective of the xenophobe. Bloom, who often appears to see only too well, is clearly not the appropriate narrator for an episode dominated by ignorance, hatred, and fear. His vision of love, despite his display of fortitude and justice, stands no chance in the hostile world of "Cyclops": "But it's no use, says he. Force, hatred, history, all that. That's not life for men and women, insult and hatred" (*U, 273*). Just as Bloom's only diversion from the depressing truth of "Sirens" is the music of the hour, his only hope in "Cyclops" is to escape the hatred and potential violence— which he and the reader manage, but through the narrative conveyance of the mock-heroic: "And they beheld Him, even Him, ben Bloom Elijah, amid clouds of angels ascend to the glory of the brightness at an angle of fortyfive degrees over Donohoe's in Little Green Street like a shot off a shovel" (*U, 283*).

After Bloom's cloudy departure in "Cyclops" the narrative next locates him at the twilight hour of "Nausicaa," though his consciousness does not recover its privileged narrative position until midepisode. In need of recreation and rest after the humiliation and insults of the past few hours, Bloom has traveled to Sandymount strand, where from a distance he observes a young woman and, provoked by her flirtation, masturbates until he reaches ejaculation. After she departs Bloom has an opportunity to put the events of the day into perspective—"Long day I've had. Martha, the bath, funeral, house of Keyes, museum with those goddesses, Dedalus' song. Then that bawler in Barney Kiernan's" (*U, 311*)—until he closes his eyes and drifts off into a state of flickering consciousness: "O sweety all your little girlwhite up I saw dirty bracegirdle made me do love sticky we two naughty Grace darling she him half past the bed met him pike hoses frillies for Raoul de perfume your wife black hair heave under embon *señorita* young eyes Mulvey plump bubs me breadvan Winkle red slippers she rusty sleep wander years of dreams return tail end Agendath swoony lovey showed me her next year in drawers return next in her next her next" (*U, 312*).

Written in what Joyce described as "a namby-pamby jammy marmalady drawersy (alto là!) style" (*Letters, 1:135*), the narrative of

"Nausicaa," after the allurement of Gerty MacDowell's consciousness and its thinly disguised performance in the language of the women's magazines of the day, returns to Bloom for a brief period of assessment and recovery preparatory to Bloom's meeting—already advertised by several near encounters—with Stephen Dedalus in the "Oxen of the Sun" episode. When, however, Bloom and Stephen finally meet in the first of Joyce's night hours, the narrative style and structure become so coated with literary scaffolding that even Joyce's most ardent critics have complained about the impenetrability of the episode. Peake, for example, claims that "the sequence of events, external or psychological, seems dominated by the historical sequence of the styles. The technique is too powerful; it overwhelms what it should serve" (Peake, 263).

When Bloom arrives at the maternity hospital to inquire about the condition of Mina Purefoy, the narrative of "Oxen of the Sun," after a Latinate invocation to fertility and birth, encloses his appearance within the language of Anglo-Saxon. As Bloom reluctantly accepts Dixon's invitation and joins a small party of medical students, includ-ing the ubiquitous Lenehan and Stephen Dedalus, the narrative, while maintaining its connection with the perceptions and thoughts of Bloom and Stephen, also begins its own movement through nine stages of literary styles until the episode concludes with the chaotic language at Burke's pub. In the episode itself Bloom, enduring the outrageous talk and behavior at the table, concerns himself with Stephen Dedalus to the point that he decides, after learning of the birth of a son to Mrs. Purefoy, to follow the crowd to Burke's. Making his first narrative appearance since "Wandering Rocks," Stephen, other than by his drunk-enness, remains unaltered in his arrogant and self-absorbed posturing, bitterness, and remorse, though Bloom, perceptive as ever, appears to recognize Stephen's vulnerability, anxiety, and uncertainty.

The various styles of "Oxen of the Sun" are comic at times in their transformation of common events—Bloom's bee sting, under the influ-ence of Malory, becomes a wound from "a horrible and dreadful dragon" (U, 317)—but for the most part they obscure the initial circumstances and effect of the long-awaited meeting between Bloom and Stephen. As the reader labors through the nine stages of literary styles, only to emerge into the chaos of shouts in the street, the narrative prevents clear recognition of what if anything has been born in the way of a new relationship, new direction, or even reaffirmation for Bloom and Ste-phen. In an episode in which prophylatics, miscarriage, death at birth, and grotesquely misshapen infants are the topics of the hour the epi-

sode's changing styles produce an uncertain vision of the meeting between Bloom and Stephen, though it does appear that the narrative, in
the announcement of a healthy birth and the emergence of Bloom and
Stephen into the Blakean chaos that concludes the episode, invites the
reader into yet another new world of possibilities: "Change here for
Bawdyhouse" (*U,* 349).

At the midnight hour, Joyce's brave new world appears out of the
murky atmosphere and surroundings of Dublin's nighttown district as
the stylistic transformations of "Oxen of the Sun" are now left behind
for the dramatic phantasmagoria of "Circe." Bloom's worries about
Stephen lead him to Bella Cohen's bawdyhouse, where both characters
face psychological showdowns with their worst thoughts and fears until
they eventually return to the streets for a physical confrontation with
the forces most dreaded and condemned by Joyce's good man and artist.
The climactic episode of the book's odyssey, "Circe," as it juxtaposes
Bloom's and Stephen's major anxieties and ordeals, also fuses the narrative's early impressionism and its later stylistic expressionism into a
dramatic form that allows conscious perceptions and thoughts and
subconscious feelings of desire and guilt to be performed on the same
plane or stage. When Zoe, described as "a young whore" in the text,
reacts to Bloom's lewdly phrased warning against the "rank weed" of
tobacco by telling him to "make a stump speech out of it" (*U,* 390), the
narrative stage of "Cyclops," as distant steeples chime the midnight
hour, overflows with the dramatic manifestations of Bloom's most secret thoughts and fantasies. Within a moment of time he becomes
creator and ruler of the new Bloomusalem, an example of the new
womanly man, and, after much abuse, martyr to his own trespasses
during his hourly travels:

Kidney of Bloom, pray for us
Flower of the Bath, pray for us
Mentor of Menton, pray for us
Canvasser for the Freeman, pray for us
Charitable Mason, pray for us
Wandering Soap, pray for us
Sweets of Sin, pray for us
Music without Words, pray for us
Reprover of the Citizen, pray for us
Friend of all Frillies, pray for us
Midwife most Merciful, pray for us
Potato Preservative against Plague and Pestilence, pray for us. (*U,* 407)

Armed with the experiences of the past hours but without his talis-
manic potato, Bloom enters the bawdyhouse, where Stephen and Lynch
are entertaining themselves. While Bloom is concerned about Stephen's
welfare, he quickly falls under the spell of the whore mistress Bella
Cohen and is threatened into swinish submission by her domineering
gaze. Though for the moment he surrenders to his darkest thoughts and
falls into the grave danger of accepting, as his lot in this dramatic hour,
the lowest and most despicable role conceivable in his own mind,
Bloom overcomes his crisis by recognizing, even in the ethereal image
of the nymph, that his innermost impulses, curiosities, and imaginings
are the common "stains" of humanity rather than a debasement of the
human spirit. Having survived his worst thoughts about himself, he
reclaims his potato: "There is a memory attached to it. I should like to
have it" (U, 453).

With Bloom's crisis ended "Circe" turns to Stephen Dedalus, whose
own odyssey through the hours reaches its climax when, in the middle of
his dance, the ghoulish image of his mother appears in full dramatic force
to claim his artistic spirit. Stephen's vulnerability, apparent throughout
the day, becomes dramatically clear when his mother warns him that for
all his claims to eternal images he too will die: "You too. Time will come"
(U, 473). Horrorstruck, Stephen begs his mother for the word, only to
hear her say, "Repent, Stephen" (U, 474). Now outraged, he defiantly
cries out in defense of the intellectual imagination—"With me all or not
at all. Non Serviam!" (U, 475)—and, refusing to submit to his own fears
and remorse, swings his ashplant against the chandelier, thereby in one
symbolic gesture shattering the temples of his youth.

Even though Bloom and Stephen have endured and overcome their
moments of crisis, the drama of the hour continues as Stephen rushes
out of the bawdyhouse and into a confrontation with two British sol-
diers. After paying for the damage to the chandelier, which actually has
suffered only a dent and broken chimney, Bloom follows Stephen into
the streets, only to watch, despite his efforts to calm the situation,
Private Carr strike Stephen in the face: "Stephen totters, collapses,
falls, stunned" (U, 491). After assuring the authorities that he will take
care of things, Bloom attends to Stephen, who in a state of flickering
consciousness mumurs fragments of lines from Yeats's "Who Goes with
Fergus?"—sung by Stephen, as he recalled in the novel's opening
episode, to his dying mother. Confused by Stephen's murmured words,
Bloom, standing "on guard," projects his own vision, now idealized, of
his dead son, Rudy, as the drama of Ulysses comes to an end.

The *Nostos,* or last three episodes of *Ulysses,* opens with "Eumaeus" and its flabby, convoluted sentences and tired, hackneyed language. Kenner, however, points out that, critical claims to the contrary, the episode itself is not boring or tired: "Joyce was never more awake than when he misaligned all those thousands of clichés" (Kenner, 130). The style in "Eumaeus" not only effectively measures the weariness of the hour and the exhausted consciousness of Bloom, which controls the episode's narrative, but also demonstrates Bloom's difficulty in communicating with Stephen and establishing some recognition of common interests. The narrative, which begins in time immediately after the "Circe" episode, follows Bloom and Stephen, who first have a brief encounter with a run-down version of the Corley of *Dubliners,* to a cabman's shelter, where they hover over a cup of coffee and a stale bun and listen to the questionable ramblings of the self-proclaimed Ulysses, D. B. Murphy. In an episode filled with confused, mistaken, or doubtful identities and undermined by the style of exhaustion Bloom spends his time futilely trying to make some connection or at least gain some measure of mutuality with a recalcitrant Stephen, even to the point of showing him a faded but revealing photograph of his wife. Only when they leave the shelter, however, does Stephen, confessing that he is "still feeling poorly and fagged out" (*U,* 539), turn in recognition of practical-minded Bloom, who then links arms with Stephen and guides him, while drawing out their common interest in music, to 7 Eccles Street for a cup of cocoa and an offer to stay the night.

Though "Eumaeus" ends with Bloom's spirit revived by all the possibilities he foresees in Stephen, the cold, mechanical catechism of the "Ithaca" episode brings the narrative back to a sobering actuality as the novel moves to its conclusion. According to Budgen, Joyce regarded "Ithaca," the "ugly duckling of the book," as his favorite episode in *Ulysses* (Budgen, 258). In a letter to Harriet Weaver Joyce had also noted that "Ithaca" is "in reality the end as *Penelope* has no beginning, middle, or end" (*Letters,* 1:172). With so much expectation and authority placed on the episode to resolve the novel, "Ithaca," while soliciting reams of information, does not offer a final union, recognition, or vision, though Joyce critics have often imposed their own solutions and resolutions on the ending of *Ulysses.* For all its stylistic curvatures the narrative bridge brings Stephen and Bloom, after a polite and friendly conversation, to a moment of departure and destiny appropriate to their separate temperaments—"The scientific. The artistic" (*U,* 558)—and circumstances—"Name, age, race, creed" (*U,* 554). Having surren-

dered the key to the Martello tower, Stephen, with no determined place
to rest for the night, still "inexplicably, with amicability, gratefully"
(*U*, 570) declines the offer to be Bloom's guest and wanders off into the
incertitude of the night. Keyless Bloom, who has found a way to return
home, takes his knowledge, confirmed by Stephen's refusal and departure, of the "irreparability" of the past—"Was the clown Bloom's son?"
(*U*, 571)—and the "imprevidibility" of the future—"Had Bloom's
coin returned?" (*U*, 571)—and retires to his now-second-best marriage
bed. In an ending that reaffirms Stephen's sense of mission in *A Portrait*
and Gabriel Conroy's need for acceptance and forgetfulness "Ithaca"
leaves Stephen to the infinite possibilities of his own genius and ambition and allows Joyce's much-traveled good man a well-earned rest.

If the "Penelope" episode is perceived as the epilogue of *Ulysses*, then
Molly Bloom has far more than the last word. Though according to
Joyce her long, flowing interior monologue has no beginning, middle,
or end, her thoughts, after being disturbed by her husband, are both a
counterpoint and a counterattraction to the narrative, just as her "last
word (human, all too human) . . . is the indispensable countersign to
Bloom's passport to eternity" (*Letters*, 1:160). Filled with outrageous
contradictions, petty sarcasms, long-standing frustrations, and blatant
ignorance, Molly's eight paragraphs—without the interruption of a
third-person narrator or even punctuation—confirm the sense of uncertainty, isolation, and resignation that ends "Ithaca." Yet despite her all-
too-human failings Molly also displays a confidence, liveliness, and joy
that gives her monologue its attractiveness and affirms the comic spirit
that has mocked Stephen's pretentiousness and Bloom's sincerity and
attended to Joyce's dance of the hours. Molly Bloom's pulsating
affirmation—"and yes I said yes I will Yes" (*U*, 644)—is the countersign to Leopold Bloom's passport to eternity, but her affirmation is
preceded by a touch of comedy—"and I thought well as well him as
another" (*U*, 643–44)—that gives the radiance of laughter to Molly's
final yes and reminds the reader of the comic triumph of *Ulysses:* its
mockery of the epic proportions or scaffolding imposed on the human
condition and its elevation of the human spirit out of the depressing
monotony of daily life.[23] In refusing to be either Homeric, *Hamlet,* or
existential stick-in-the-mud, *Ulysses* becomes one of the great achievements in modern literature.

Chapter Five
Refined out of Existence: Lots of Fun at *Finnegans Wake*

Stephen Dedalus concludes his discussion of literary forms with a radiant vision of the artist reaching his highest achievement in an aesthetic image so "purified in and reprojected from the human imagination" that the artist's personality "finally refines itself out of existence, impersonalises itself" (*P*, 215). C. H. Peake, in his discussion of *A Portrait*, points out that Stephen's claim is for more than artistic indifference, detachment, or isolation: "Like God, the artist is not only behind, beyond and above his handiwork, but also within it. His personality is refined out of existence because it is, like God's, embodied in his creation. Instead of love and hate, there is a universal creative vitality; instead of personal sympathy, there is a more complete and general sympathy flowing into every person. The condition of artistic creation in the dramatic form is a detachment of the spirit from personal concerns in order that there may be a universal penetration into all the concerns of the created world" (Peake, 89). Peake's defense of Stephen's aesthetic handiwork, while giving credibility to Stephen's much-maligned theorizing, is also a fitting description of the direction of Joyce's art after the completion of *Ulysses*. Instead of turning to the dramatic form Joyce made the epilogue of *Ulysses* a prelude to a new form that would also have no beginning, middle, or end; but his creation after *Ulysses* would be, like Stephen's dramatic form, a universal penetration rather than a further expression of personal concerns and epic dimensions. The new work, once in progress, would also require a new language and scaffold as well as a radically new concept of character and setting to express the creative vitality and sympathetic flow of Joyce's cosmic vision of the relationship between the word and the world.

Finnegans Wake

As artists and critics reacted to *Ulysses*, often with puzzlement or astonishment but sometimes with disgust, and as public authorities condemned and banned the book, Joyce began the 16-year ordeal of writing *Finnegans Wake:* "Complications to right of me, complications to left of me, complex on the page before me, perplex in the pen beside me, duplex in the meandering eyes of me, stuplex on the face that reads me. And from time to time I lie back and listen to my hair growing white" *(Letters,* 1:222). Having written his book of the day by hanging the hourly wanderings of Stephen Dedalus and Leopold Bloom on a mythical structure corresponding to Homer's *Odyssey,* he planned his book of the night around Giordano Bruno's theory of contraries and Giambattista Vico's theory of the cyclical patterns of history: "I would not pay overmuch attention to these theories, beyond using them for all they are worth, but they have gradually forced themselves on me through circumstances of my own life. I wonder where Vico got his fear of thunderstorms" *(Letters,* 1:241). To write the book, however, Joyce, who had already experimented with language and style in the waking night hours of *Ulysses,* needed a language, characters, and narrative appropriate for the hours of sleep and dream: "One great part of every human existence is passed in a state which cannot be rendered sensible by the use of wideawake language, cutanddry grammar and goahead plot" *(Letters,* 3:146).

To emphasize Joyce's rejection of "goahead" diction, syntax, and plot, *Finnegans Wake* "ends in the middle of a sentence and begins in the middle of the same sentence" *(Letters,* 1:246). Yet the in-between world of the *Wake* is founded upon the improbable, go-ahead narrative of an Irish ballad, "Finnegan's Wake," which also lends its title to Joyce's book. In the ballad Tim Finnegan, an Irish hod carrier who has "a sort of tipplin way," falls from a ladder and breaks his skull. At the wake, however, Tim is revived during a brawl when whiskey is accidentally scattered on his corpse. Rising from his bed, Tim Finnegan cries out, "Do you think I'm dead?"[1] By removing the apostrophe from the title of the ballad, Joyce created, in a book riddled with jokes, puzzles, and games, the first pun in *Finnegans Wake.* With no indicator of the possessive, the wake of Finnegan becomes just its contrary: the rising of Finnegans everywhere, including, of course, Tim Finnegan, who after all is resurrected in the popular ballad. Tim Finnegan, the titled character of Joyce's book, also appears in the opening pages of *Finnegans Wake* as "Bygmester Finnegan"[2]—the pun on *burgomaster* gives Finnegan both great size and authority—though his figure, like the ballad itself, undergoes embellishment and extension. Finnegan's fall is mourned by "all the hoolivans of the nation, prostrated in their consternation" *(FW,* 6.15–

16), and honored at a wake appropriate to a "dacent gaylabouring youth" (*FW*, 6.23) who, in Joyce's *Wake,* is also transformed into the great hero of Irish legend, Finn MacCool—"Macool, Macool, orra whyi deed ye diie? of a trying thirstay mournin" (*FW*, 6.13–14)—and a biblical "behemoth" (*FW*, 7.14) capable of feeding the multitudes if they can hold him down. Later in the first chapter of the *Wake* Finnegan, this time appearing as "Mr. Finnimore" (*FW*, 24.16), rises at the mention of the words "Wake" and "Usqueadbaugham" (*FW*, 24.14), a Wakean variation of the Irish word for whiskey, only to be assured that he can take his "laysure like a God on pension" (*FW*, 24.16–17) because he will be honored and remembered as "ultimendly respunchable for the hubbub caused in Edenborough" (*FW*, 29.29).

The metamorphosis of Tim Finnegan, an Irish hod carrier, into the biblical Adam, the legendary MacCool, and the Master Builder of civilizations, together with the transformation of an outrageous Irish ballad into a continuous narrative of the fall and rise of the human race, from Original Sin through modern warfare, appears as fragments in Joyce's night book of human history. To bring all of history into play Joyce turned to Vico's *Scienza Nuova* and adopted for his own purposes Vico's axioms on ideal eternal history. For the *Wake*'s structure, or what Joyce called the book's "trellis,"[3] he borrowed Vico's idea of human history continuously moving through three ages—the age of gods, the age of heroes, and the age of men—but extended Vico's idea of a *ricorso*—a thunderclap announcing the birth of a new cycle of ages— into a brief fourth age, or structural unit. According to Clive Hart, Joyce "still adheres to the general Viconian progress—Birth, Marriage, Death, and Reconstitution—but the *ricorso,* which in Vico is little more than a transitional flux, is given as much prominence as the other Ages and is even elevated to the supreme moment of the cycle."[4]

The Vichian trellis of *Finnegans Wake* is apparent in its division into four books, christened by Joseph Campbell and Henry Morton Robinson, in their *A Skeleton Key to "Finnegans Wake,"* as the Book of the Parents, the Book of the Sons, the Book of the People, and the Recorso,[5] and the further division of each of the first three books into either two groupings of four chapters (Book I) or four chapters (Books II and III), with the fourth book, or *ricorso,* appropriately standing alone as a final or transitional chapter. A book with no beginning, middle, or end, *Finnegans Wake,* in the revolving structure of its four books and 17 chapters, finds reinforcement in the idea of history endlessly moving through cyclical patterns. Vichian cycles also appear, however, within books and chapters, even within paragraphs and sentences: "eggburst, eggblend, eggburial, and hatch-as-hatch can" (*FW,* 614.32–33). Moreover, Vico's further theory that each historical cycle has not only its own nature but its own wisdom, language, customs, laws, and institutions finds its way into the language, themes, and characters of *Finnegans Wake.*[6]

The first chapter of the *Wake* often presents Finnegan and his fall in divine, gigantic, or parental proportions: "The great fall . . . prumptly sends an unquiring one well to the west in quest of his tumptytumtoes" (*FW,* 3.20–21). Even the appearance in the first chapter of two Dublin barflies, contemporaries of the cartoon characters Mutt and Jeff, is transformed into an encounter between the prehistoric Mutt and Jute, though out of their struggle to swap names, identities, and stories, the more articulate Mutt recognizes and tries to express the cylical nature of time and events: "This ourth of years is not save brickdust and being humus the same roturns. He who runes may rede it on all fours" (*FW,* 18.3–5). Mutt's last statement is particularly provocative, not only because it draws attention to Vico's four ages and leaves Jute "thonthorstrok" (*FW,* 18.16) but also because it appears to set in motion, in its pun on writing, reading, and speaking, the first alphabet, the beginning of another round of Vichian cycles, and perhaps the telling of multiple tales of Finnegan: "(Stoop) if you are abcedminded, to this claybook, what curios of signs (please stoop), in this allaphbed! Can you rede (since We and Thou had it out already) its world? It is the same told of all. Many. Miscegenations on miscegenations. Tieckle. They lived und laughed ant loved end left. Forsin. . . . The meandertale, aloss and again, of our old Heidenburgh in the days when Head-in-Clouds walked the earth" (*FW,* 18.17–24).

Within the Vichian structure of *Finnegans Wake* Joyce's characters, or "the centuple celves of my egourge as Micholas de Cusack calls them" (*FW* 49.33–34), appear to shape themselves and move according to Bruno's "coincidance of their contraries" (*FW,* 49.36). Joyce admired Bruno long before writing *Finnegans Wake* and used his theory to good effect in developing the coincidental encounters in *Ulysses* between contraries like Boylan and Bloom and, of course, Bloom and Stephen.[7] In *Finnegans Wake,* however, identities, relationships, and even words dance with their contraries. The central character of the *Wake,* though recognized by the book's title and ballad as Finnegan, actually has so many identities, including his contemporary manifestation as the pubkeeper Humphrey Chimpden Earwicker, that he is commonly recognized and

referred to by the initials HCE—which signify, among many things, his
universality, "Here Comes Everybody" (*FW,* 32.18–19); his humanity,
"human, erring, and condonable" (*FW,* 58.19); his paternity, "Haveth
Childers Everywhere" (*FW,* 535.34–35); his variety, "Heinz cans everywhere" (*FW,* 581.05); and even his guilty stutter, "HeCitEncy" (*FW,*
421.23); or, if the initials are reversed, his capacities for resurrection, re-
sumption, and restoration, "erect, confident and heroic" (*FW,* 619.14).[8]

Anna Livia Plurabelle, HCE's female counterpart, shares his humanity and universality in her various manifestations and roles in *Finnegans
Wake.* Also more commonly known by her initials, ALP must defend her
husband's shaky authority and reputation against a multitude of accusers
and slanderers: "Stringstly is it forbidden by the honorary tenth com-
mendmant to shall not bare full sweetness against a nighboor's wiles"
(*FW,* 615.32–33). She also has the responsibility for preserving the truth
about HCE or about human history and for providing hope for future
generations: "Here, and it goes on to appear now, she comes, a
peacefugle, a parody's bird, a peri potmother, a pringlpik in the
ilandiskippy, with peewee and powwows in beggybaggy on her bicky-
backy and a flick flask fleckflinging its pixylighting pacts' huemeramy-
bows" (*FW,* 11.08–12). As her name suggests, she has the singularity of
Anna, the constancy of Livia—the name connotes the river Liffey—and
the maternity of Plurabelle. She also, like Molly Bloom, has the final say
and the last word of the book: "End here. Us then. Finn, again! Take.
Bussoftlhee, mememormee! Till thousendsthee. Lps. The keys to.
Given! A way a lone a last a loved a long the (*FW,* 628.13–16)—but
ALP's flowing nature, even as she appears to be fading out, carries the
reader back to the first word of the book, the beginning of another cycle,
and, of course, to HCE: "riverrun, past Eve and Adam's, from swerve of
shore to bend of bay, brings us by a commodius vicus of recirculation
back to Howth Castle and Environs" (*FW,* 3.01–03).

While HCE and ALP have children everywhere, the *Wake* family
limits itself to the manifestations of male twins and a daughter.
Though assuming various names and roles, the twins are most commonly recognized as Shem and Shaun and the daughter as Issy. As
twins, Shem and Shaun are as capable of trading identities and places as
Tristopher and Hilary, the "two little jiminies" of the prankquean tale
and the answer to her riddle, "why do I am alook a poss of porterpease"
(*FW,* 21.18–19). As Shem and Shaun, however, the twins validate
Bruno's coincidence of contraries in their opposite personalities and
their hostility toward each other despite Issy's peacemaking efforts. The

children are capable of an alliance, but only in subverting the authority of HCE. Oddly enough, when they are engaged in a conflict of generations the males become three antagonists—"the three lipoleum boyne grouching down in the living detch" (FW, 8.21–22)—and the female becomes two—"a pair of dainty maidservants in the swoolth of the rushy hollow" (FW 34.19–20)—whether the conflict be a composite of history's wars or the notorious incident in the park.

The Shem figure in the Wake is an obvious extension of Joyce's autobiographical portrait of the artist into new dimensions of self-parody: "Shem is as short for Shemus as Jem is joky for Jacob" (FW, 169.01). Joyce readers frustrated with the posturing of Stephen Dedalus in A Portrait and Ulysses should be delighted with the Shaunian-inspired description and account of Shem as the grotesquely formed, because he takes his shape from figures of speech, answer to "the first riddle of the universe: asking, when is a man not a man. . . . the correct solution being—all give it up?—; when he is a—yours till the rending of the rocks,—Sham" (FW, 170.04–05, 23–24). Blasphemous, debauched, cowardly, Shem, the "fraid born fraud" (FW, 172.21), is mocked as the author of "inartistic portraits of himself" (FW, 182.19), "his usylessly unreadable Blue Book of Eccles" (FW, 179.26–27), and "one continuous present tense integument slowly unfolded all marryvoising moodmoulded cyclewheeling history" (FW, 185–86, 36–02). Joyce's artist in the Wake is also accused of telling "nameless shamelessness about everybody ever he met" (FW, 182.13); of being "self exiled in upon his ego" (FW, 184.06–07); of creating his art out of his own excrement and, rejected by publishers, of writing his "obscene matter . . . over every square inch of the only foolscap available, his own body" (FW, 185.30–36); and of forcing "an epical forged cheque on the public for his own private profit" (FW, 181.16–17).

Shem's accuser, the industrious and respectable Shaun, presents himself as the perfect contrary to his mad brother, though the subversive language of Finnegans Wake continually undermines his claims to perfection while exposing his pomposity. In The Mime of Mick, Nick, and the Maggies Shaun, in the dramatis persona of Chuff, is described as "the fine frank fairhaired fellow of the fairytales" (FW, 220.12–13), a stark contrast to Shemese Glugg, "the bold bad bleak boy of the storybooks" (FW, 219.24). Shaun's principal role in the Wake is to deliver the synecdoche letter that will tell all about the family, that is, if anyone can read or understand its writing: "Wind broke it. Wave bore it. Reed wrote of it. Syce run with it. Hand tore it and wild went war. Hen trieved it and plight pledged peace. It was folded with cunning, sealed with crime, uptied by a harlot, undone by a child. It was life but was it fair? It was free but was it art?" (*FW,* 94.05–10). Swelled with his own immensity, Shaun eventually if reluctantly goes about his rounds, comparable in the Wakean landscape to the stations of the cross, but he also takes it upon himself, as an eminent spatialist, to lecture on the time-space controversy; to offer up, as moral authority, his own commandments on the proper conduct for young girls; to condemn, as a most reluctant brother's keeper, Shem's irresponsible and fraudulent behavior; and to deliver, as his father's son, his own psyche to an inquiry into HCE's alleged sins and crimes: "His dream monologue was over, of cause, but his drama parapolylogic had yet to be, affact" (*FW,* 474.04–05).

Issy does not appear in *Finnegans Wake* as often as her brothers, but she has an important role in relationship to each member of her family. In The Mime of Mick, Nick, and the Maggies she plays Izod: "a bewitching blonde who dimples delightfully and is approached in loveliness only by her grateful sister reflection in a mirror" (*FW,* 220.07–09). Infatuated by her own mirror image, Issy also plays the flirtatious lure for HCE's manifestations as the old fool and becomes both a distraction and a comforter to Shem and Shaun: "She tried all the winsome wonsome ways her four winds had taught her" (*FW,* 157.30–32). Alice to her mirror and Iseult to the men in her life, Issy is also, however, her mother's daughter, and though she may appear as a winsome little cloud or as "dadad's lottiest daughter pearl and brooder's cissiest auntybride" (*FW,* 561.15–16) she inevitably, within the cyclical movement of the *Wake,* inherits ALP's knowledge and her life: "If you spun your yarns to him on the swishbarque waves I was spelling my yearns to her over cottage cake" (FW, 620.34–36).

The *Wake* family, which Issy in an irreverent footnote both reduces to and abstracts into the Doodles family,[9] also has a supporting cast, including the inquisitive four old men, often associated, as Mamalujo, with the four gospelers; the jurors or customers, depending on HCE's predicament or condition; the 29 rainbow girls, counting the leap-girl Issy; and poor old Joe and Kate, drudgelike characters who perform the odd jobs in *Finnegans Wake.* This "collideorscape" (*FW,* 143.28) of "Morphios" and "maggies" (*FW,* 142.29–30) is, however, merely a variegated extension of HCE, ALP, and their children, who in turn are figments of the "dream aesthetic" of *Finnegans Wake,* though not necessarily the fabrications of a single dream or dreamer.[10]

Unlike *A Portrait* and *Ulysses, Finnegans Wake*, though it has the artist figure in Shem, does not offer the reader a direct discussion of aesthetics similar to Stephen's theories on apprehension, form, and the creative imagination. The *Wake* does, however, have its letter, and in the midst of unreliable witnesses, unsubstantiated charges, and contradictory rumors and accounts of the whereabouts of HCE the letter becomes the reader's best hope for the "Last Only True Account" (*FW*, 107.01–02) of HCE. Accordingly, after the kaleidoscopic opening chapter, followed by three murky chapters filled with rumors and accusations, even the characters in the *Wake* cry out for "the letter! The litter! And the soother the bitther!" (*FW*, 93.24).

The next chapter, the fifth in the book, responds to the growing confusion and the desperate plea for help by offering a reader's guide to the letter and, by extension, to *Finnegans Wake* itself. Not surprisingly, the chapter opens with a prayer to ALP, who has the responsibility for restoring, preserving, and protecting the letter, and with the initial discovery that the "mamafesta" (*FW*, 104.04) is untitled, though it "has gone by many names at disjointed times" (*FW*, 104.04–05). Since the first conundrum of the letter is its title, the guide chapter catalogs the letter's previous names, which include numerous puns on several tales within the *Wake*, perhaps as hints or lures for the frustrated reader.[11]

After the catalog of titles the chapter calls attention to the "proteiform" of the letter itself, a "polyhedron of scripture" (*FW*, 107.08) that, depending on the perspective, appears to be either "a very sexmosaic" (*FW*, 107.06) or "the purest kidooleyoon" (*FW*, 107.19). Under close inspection the letter becomes an inventory of "a multiplicity of personalities" (*FW*, 107.24–25), though when eyes close "the *chiaroscuro* coalesce, their contrarieties eliminated, in one stable somebody" (*FW*, 107.29–30) who bumps along "down the long lane of . . . generations, more generations and still more generations" (*FW*, 107.34–35). To arrive, however, at some illumination of the text and its authorship, the reader is advised to have "patience: and remember patience is the great thing, and above all things else we must avoid anything like being or becoming out of patience" (*FW*, 108.08–10).

The need for patience becomes clear as the *Wake* reader, already frustrated by the protean form of the letter, is advised to look at the "enveloping facts" rather than "the psychological content" (*FW*, 109.13–14) and at the "few artifacts" (*FW*, 110.01) or fragments that are still recognizable or readable. This Aristotelian strategy, which gives Stephen's aesthetics their intellectual foundation, appears, however, to have only marginal success, in that it produces out of "a few spontaneous fragments" (FW, 110.29) a fragmented, distorted, badly stained version of the letter. Unfortunately, even "Harrystotalies" is destabilized in *Finnegans Wake*, where the Aristotelian possible-made-possible has become the possible-made-"the improbable and the improbable the inevitable" (*FW*, 110.12).

Since the best that an Aristotelian can offer is to identify the fragments and explain what probably happened to make a mess of the "micromass" (*FW*, 111.28) of the letter, the reader still feels lost in a "jungle of woods. . . . Bethicket me for a stump of a beech if I have the poultriest notions what the farest he all means" (*FW*, 112.04–06). To get a poultry notion the reader turns to the Wakean gatherer of artifacts, the old Biddy of the battlefield, for an explanation, but all that "schwants" to "schwrites" (*FW*, 113.12) is an apology for the "old story" of HCE's alleged misconduct. The reader, still in search of a poultry notion, is then turned from a cock-and-hen story to "straight turkey" (*FW*, 113.26) talk from twin Bruno scholars, who apply both eye and ear to the text, only to discover "lines of litters slittering up and louds of latters slettering down" (*FW*, 114.17–18).

Still in search of meaning—"where in the waste is the wisdom?" (*FW*, 114.20)—the reader, after observing the stains on the letter, is advised to seek out "the identities in the writer complexus" (*FW*, 115.33), even though the letter, a perfect signature in itself, is unsigned. Understanding the writer's complexes, however, leads the reader into the wonderland of psychological criticism and an encounter with "we grisly old Sykos who have done our unsmiling bit on 'alices, when they were yung and easily freudened" (*FW*, 115.21–24). Once the writer's complexes are probed by Jungians and Freudians, they are decodified for the reader by Marxist critics, who find "that Father Michael about this red time of the white terror equals the old regime and Margaret is the social revolution" (FW, 116.07–08).

With matters growing more complex, the reader, assured that the letter actually signifies the same old story—"The olold stoliolum" (*FW*, 117.11), told through Vichian cycles, of human coincidence and conflict—turns to the signifiers themselves, the sentences, words, and letters, for illumination, since the letter "is not a miseffectual whyacinthinous riot of blots and blurs and bars and balls and hoops and wriggles and juxtaposed jottings linked by spurts of speed: it only looks as like it as damn it" (*FW*, 118.28–31). The "noodle swim or sink" task of studying the art of the copyist is for the "ideal reader suffering from an ideal insomnia" (FW, 120.13–14), but the approach appears to have the potential, as if in compensation for the reader's eyestrain, for yielding something of the learning, talent, and virtues of our copyist, as well as his excesses and flaws, and for providing the close reader with some interesting puzzles and quiet amusement. While the letter may not be "funferal" (FW, 120.10), it has at least attracted the grave professors, who have added their own markings to the "original document" (FW, 123.33–34). Their probing, the "numerous stabs and foliated gashes made by a pronged instrument" (FW, 124.02–03), may, however, hinder as much as help the reader.[12]

The chapter on the letter has anticipated a great deal of the controversy and criticism about Finnegans Wake. Even as the book was in progress Joyce's readers puzzled over the fragments and questioned the sense of it all, while Joyce urged them to have patience, guided them through their early frustrations, and lured them on with various conundrums, including, of course, guessing the title. Since the book's publication Wake criticism has gone through its own cycles and generated its own controversies.[13] While some readers have burrowed into the Wake to find meaning in the explication of certain passages, others have looked at the surface for form and structure.[14] While some scholars have identified the books and characters of the Wake and provided comprehensive lexicons and annotations, others have questioned the relevance of searching for narrative, character, and meaning. For every critic who pleads for a simple reading of Finnegans Wake to discover its constructive powers, there is another critic who urges the reader to recognize the decentering, or reductive, tendencies of the Wake.[15]

While the chapter on the letter aptly illustrates the maddening demands on the reader of Finnegans Wake, the swirling and conflicting critical claims about the Wake suggest that Joyce at least provided ample dimensions in the book for lots of fun. Professor Jones, Wyndham Lewis, and the Ondt to the contrary, Finnegans Wake gives the reader both the time and the space to hear a good story, even if the telling is a variation on or a recycling of a familiar tale. The book also allows the reader to see the familiar world through the prism of multiple perspectives that often appear both infinitely regressive and infinitely expansive to the reader's eye. To attend upon Joyce's Wake, then, becomes a task fit for an Einstein rather than the common reader. To read a word, line, or page of the Wake requires both the eye and the ear, as well as an interest or willingness to explicate details and play on the surface. The book seemingly invites diachronic and synchronic readings and assumes that the impossible—the simultaneous conjunction of time and space, eye and ear, explication and scanning, construction and deconstruction—is now not only possible but expected and the source of the fun in the night world of *Finnegans Wake.*

The multidimensional, multilinguistic journey through *Finnegans Wake* parallels the epic and stylistic adventures of *Ulysses,* but the reader's experience is not so much an odyssey as a descent into wonderland or a trip through the looking glass. The first words, sentences, and paragraphs of the *Wake* present a world in which conventional assumptions about language, narrative, character, and dimension are immediately undermined. At the beginning the *Wake* reader may even protest and claim, as does Alice in response to a letter of nonsense verses, that "I don't believe there's an atom of meaning in it." Once inside the *Wake,* however, the reader, may, like the King, see the advantage and the humor in all the nonsense—"If there's no meaning in it . . . that saves a world of trouble, you know, as we needn't try to find any"— though even the King, by spreading out the verses and taking a closer look, admits, "I seem to see meaning in them after all."

The first sentence of *Finnegans Wake,* which according to Joyce is in effect also the continuation of the last sentence of the book, transforms the traditional narrative opening of "once upon a time" into an invitation by "recirculation" (*FW,* 03.01) to its current landscape: "to Howth Castle and Environs" (*FW,* 03.02–03). The next two sentences, which also make up the first complete paragraph of the *Wake,* appear, like the first page of *A Portrait,* to contain the book's major themes, or in this case the most recurring events or commonly found artifacts of human history. These Wakean artifacts suggest a history of human conflict over sex and politics—"to wielderfight his penisolate war" (*FW,* 03.06)—economics and religion—"avoice from afire bellowsed mishe mishe to tauftauf thuartpeatrick" (*FW,* 03.09–10)—and family and generation—"a kidscad buttended a bland old isaac" (*FW,* 03.10–11)—that after a period of pause and refreshment recircles to begin again—"regginbrow was to be seen ringsome on the aquaface" (*FW,* 03.14).

The next paragraph announces, with the appropriate clarion of the *Wake*'s first thunder word, the inevitable result of all this human conflict: "The fall (bababadalgharaghtakamminarronnkonnbronntonnerronntuonnthunntrovarrhounawnskawntoohoohoordenenthurnuk!) of a once wallstrait oldparr is retaled early in bed and later on life down through all christian minstrelsy" (*FW,* 03.15–18). Not surprisingly, the fall and its aftershocks—"Killykillkilly: a toll, a toll" (*FW*, 04.07–08)—are to be followed by a rise—"Phall if you but will, rise you must" (*FW*, 04.15–16). Before, however, the awakening of a new day, life, or cycle or before the *Wake* comes to its own "setdown secular phoenish" (*FW*, 04.17) the book takes the reader on an inquest into the subject of the fall and an inquiry into the agent that "brought about that tragoady thundersday this municipal sin business" (*FW*, 05.13–14).

The beginning of the inquest or the inquiry has the potential for generating narrative moment, character development, plot twists, and a proper denouement, but in actuality the strategy of *Finnegans Wake* is to exploit the modes of inquiry and the reader's curiosity. Instead of narrative movement the reader listens to rumor and gossip, finds fragmented or distorted writings, and hears variation on variation of what appears to be a familiar story. Rather than encountering conventional protagonists and antagonists the reader encounters characters with elusive identities, multiple personalities, and interchangeable parts. As for plot, *Finnegans Wake*, like an inquiry, seems to be going somewhere, but, unlike a novel, it has language and movement that create the appearance of being simultaneously multidimensional and multidirectional.

The first chapter of *Finnegans Wake*, though difficult for the reader, is also an excellent exercise for reading the entire book. Once the inquiry is called for, the reader immediately learns that there is a chorus of stories, told through the ages, about the fall: "There extand by now one thousand and one stories, all told, of the same" (*FW*, 05.28–29). After hearing a few rumors and a distorted chorus or two from the ballad of Tim Finnegan, the reader is given "a proudseye view" (*FW*, 07.36) of the "brontoichthyan form" (*FW*, 07.20), though in the transformative world of the *Wake* the "mounding's mass" turns out to be the "Willingdone Museyroom" (*FW*, 08.10). The trip to the Museyroom begins a round of inspecting battlefield artifacts, encountering odd and sometimes-sinister characters like Mutt and Jute, hearing stories filled with pranks and riddles, and even comforting and reassuring the fallen giant so that he does not rise prematurely. As the first cycle of *Finnegans Wake* comes to an end the reader, after sorting through various pieces and sources of information and rumor, is led to one possible conclusion. Having provoked the human conflicts that set in motion the cycles of history, as evidenced in the museyroom, and having engendered the coincidence of contraries, as related in the tale of the prankquean and confirmed in the confrontation between Mutt and Jute, the gigantic form—whether Finnegan, Willingdone, or Jarl Van Hoother—is "ultimendly respunchable for the hubbub caused in Edenborough" (*FW*, 29.35–36)—the buried initials HCE, once uncovered, are a dead giveaway.

The second chapter of Book I deepens and expands the inquiry into the fall, but, as the reader burrows and scans for the truth, the investigation encounters more and more embellishments, complications, and uncertainties as the subject under scrutiny grows more and more dense and foggy. The chapter begins as if in response to a specific inquiry "concerning the genesis of Harold or Humphrey Chimpden's occupational agnomen" (*FW*, 30.02–03). Even though the reader is "told how in the beginning it came to pass" (*FW*, 30.12), the actual story of how Earwicker got his name, as Michael Begnal has well illustrated, is so thickly embellished that *Wake* commentators have come up with different versions, though most agree "that the Earwicker family got its name because its forebearer was associated with an insect, the earwig" (Begnal, 11).

The difficulty of understanding the Earwicker story is further complicated by questions raised concerning its historical accuracy, though the reader is assured that "The great fact emerges that after that historic date all holographs so far exhumed initialled by Haromphrey bear the sigla H.C.E." (*FW*, 32.12–14) and that the populace "gave him as sense of those normative letters the nickname Here Comes Everybody" (*FW*, 32.18–19). This information confirms what the observant reader already knows, that the story of the fall is earmarked on practically every page with the sigla HCE. The characters of the sigla, however, rather than clarifying matters, set off another round of rumor, slander, and accusations that eventually provokes, after another thunder word, "The Ballad of Persse O'Reilly." In the ballad HCE is vilified for his failings and fallings and is accused of various "trash, tricks and trumpery" (*FW*, 46.06). The ballad, finding nothing redeemable about HCE, buries his reputation and concludes:

> And not all the king's men nor his horses
> Will resurrect his corpus
> For there's no true spell in Connacht or hell
> (bis) That's able to raise a Cain. (*FW*, 47.26–29)

One of the most intriguing pieces from HCE's shattered reputation appears to have something to do with an incident in the park involving two young girls and three boys. The search in the third chapter for a fuller explanation of "the haardly creditable edventyres of the Haberdasher, the two Curchies and the three Enkelchums in their Bearskin ghoats" (*FW*, 51.14–15) is, however, hampered by the dense fog covering the chapter and the disappearance of those responsible for the ballad. Nevertheless, the inquiry continues through another round of encounters with more "evidencegivers by leg poll to untrustworthily irreperible" and others only too willing to pass judgment on HCE— like the girl detective Sylvia Silence, who when supplied with "the several facets of the case" asks if it is possible that "sheew gweatness was his twadgedy" (*FW*, 61.03, 07). The chapter appears to be making some progress—"But resuming inquiries" (*FW*, 66.10). . . . "To proceed" (*FW*, 67.07). . . . "Now to the obverse" (*FW*, 67.28). . . . "Now by memory inspired" (*FW*, 69.05). . . . "O, by the by" (*FW*, 69.30)—but other than embellishing another incident in the park— the "alleged misdemeanour" between HCE and "a cad with a pipe" (*FW*, 35.06, 011) that inspired the ballad—the only result by chapter's end is "a long list (now feared in part lost) to be kept on file of all abusive names he was called" (*FW*, 71.05–06). The list rivals the ballad in its scurrilous attack on HCE, yet it still encloses its abuse within the context of the rise—"Firstnighter" (*FW*, 71.10)—and the fall— "deposed" (*FW*, 72.16).

The ballad and the partial catalog of abusive names fail to awaken an answer or solution to the *Wake*, but the incidents in the park suggest that the fallen HCE did something to someone to get in his present situation and that somebody did something to him to send him into hiding or hibernation. In the fourth chapter, which concludes the book's first cycle, the inquiry into HCE's character and condition follows up earlier leads, circles around previous accounts, listens to the latest unreliable testimony, and, after another exhaustive hunt, concludes that the matter is so many-sided that the next round of "Notes and queries" (*FW*, 101.04–05) should be directed at the "one nearer him, dearer than all, first warming creature of his early morn, bondwoman of the man of the house, and murrmurr of all the mackavicks" (*FW*, 101.31–33).

The appeal to ALP produces the chapter on the letter but also widens the circle of inquiry by turning to a member of HCE's family. The fifth chapter also begins a new cycle of inquiries that include a close inspection of the family letter; 12 questions covering the HCE household and homestead; an account, delivered by Shaun, of his brother Shem; and finally all the gossip being spread about ALP. After four chapters, then, that set into motion a frustrating, confusing, inconclusive search for the identity of HCE and the cause of his fall, the next four chapters, comprising a second book within Book I of the *Wake,* lead the reader to the family and to another round of burrowing and scanning, though this time the Wakean multiple lens focuses on circumstance rather than occasion or event.

Though the chapter on the letter functions for the most part as a parodic reader's guide to *Finnegans Wake* itself, it also reveals that the letter, despite its grotesquely distorted condition, contains "all sorts of horsehappy values and masses of meltwhile horse" (*FW,* 111.29–30) and appears to have something to do with the family cycle: "allathome's health well . . . wedding cakes . . . grand funferrall . . . fondest to the twoinns" (*FW,* 111.11–17). Accordingly, the reader encounters in the next chapter "a nightly quisquiquock" of 12 questions, prepared by Shem and delivered by Shaun, on the Wakean family and its environs. Appropriately, the first question asks for the identity of the head of the family—"the first to rise taller" (*FW,* 126.11). The elusive subject of all inquiries, he has already been "variously catalogued, regularly regrouped" (*FW,* 129.12) and been known to move in "vicous circles yet remews the same" (*FW,* 134.16–17). The question, which in itself becomes an extended catalog with its own various cycles, does finally lead to an answer, which in this case is the manifestation of HCE as the Irish mythical hero Finn MacCool. Now that "our awful dad" (*FW,* 136.21) has been identified as mythical, heroic, and Irish—characteristics that correspond to Vico's cycles—the questioning turns to HCE's mate: "Does your mutter know your mike?" (*FW,* 139.14). While the question mocks the paternalism of a father possessed by multiple identities, it also mirrors the inquiry's earlier appeal to ALP. The answer in turn confirms that ALP, having "slipt by his side" (*FW,* 139.18–19), knows HCE and, despite his many manifestations and roundabout behavior, remains adjustable, loyal, and patient—"Amin!" (*FW,* 139.28).

After questions on the parents, the family quiz, arranged and conducted by the children, moves on to HCE's environs. A question on the family motto provokes an outrageous pun on the city of Dublin's motto—"Obedienta civium urbis Felicitas"—and on HCE's size—"Thine obesity, O civilian, hits the felicitude of our orb!" (*FW,* 140.06–07). The motto leads the reader to a further question, asking for the name of the "Irish capitol city" (*FW,* 140.08), which, in spite of

blatant hints, is variously identified as Ireland's provincial capitals:
"Delfas. . . . Dorhqk. . . . Nublid. . . . Dalway" (FW, 140.15, 21,
27, 36).

With the family homestead loosely located in Irish environs, though
hints are that the pub, mound, or letter lies close to Dublin, the quiz
whirls through the manifestations of the supporting or perhaps surrounding cast of Wakean characters—the hired help, the customers,
the temptresses—only to arrive at the usual dizzying perspective and
question—"*what* would that fargazer seem to seemself to seem seeming
of, dimm it all?" (FW, 143.26–27)—and the same old contradictory
and prismatic answer—"A collideorscape" (FW, 143.28). While the
last three questions do nothing to simplify, solidify, or solve the book's
inquiry, they at least illustrate key characteristics of the human folly
that leads to the fall and the human conflicts that reverberate throughout history in the aftermath. They also lead the quiz, as well as the
direction of the inquiry, to the children.

The tenth question turns the reader's attention to love and desire,
but the appeal to "shee that draws" (FW, 143.29) yields only a long,
rambling monologue of a young girl, self-absorbed with her own
charms, who flirts, teases, and tempts both young and old: "It's only
because the rison is I'm only any girl you lovely fellow of my dreams,
and because old somebooby is not a roundabout" (FW, 146.05–06).
The penultimate question of the quiz shifts the reader's attention from
the temptation of Issy's "amor andmore" (FW, 148.31) to the resulting
conflict between the brothers. When asked if he is willing to be his
brother's keeper Shaun assumes a professorial voice to lecture on the
impossibility of opposites merging. A spatialist by nature, he rejects
the temporal arguments of "Bitchson" (FW, 149.20) and "Winestain"
(FW, 149.28). He, then, illustrates his position with the "old fabulist's
parable" (FW, 152.13) of the Mookse and the Gripes and the political
account of Burrus and Caseous. Intolerant of antipathies, Shaun, as
evident in the quiz's last question, judges Shem both a disgrace and a
curse.

The accusation against Shem and the possibility that he is behind the
reader's current nightmare lead the inquiry to a chapter on Shem and
give Shaun the opportunity to elaborate on his hateful brother. The
inquiry now turns into an inquisition, as Shaun mercilessly brands Shem
a coward, liar, drunk, and fraud. As the artist, Shem is attacked for his
shameless, gross productions—he creates out of the "obscene matter"
(FW, 185.30) of his own body. Because he slanders the family he is also

condemned for "adding to the already unhappiness of this our popeyed world" (*FW*, 189.09–10). Eventually taking on the role of Justius, Shaun builds toward the only conclusion possible from his perspective, that his brother is mad and must be sentenced, because he is the artist, to silence: "He points the deathbone and the quick are still" (*FW*, 193.29).

As Mercius, Shem closes out the chapter with a brief defense appropriate to the artist. He begins with a confession that is as much boastful defiance as self-accusation—"Pariah, cannibal Cain" (*FW*, 193.32)—but his real defense is his artistry, his ability to lift "the lifewand and the dumb speak" (*FW*, 195.05). This ability, well illustrated by Shem's mimicry of ALP, carries the reader on the rhetorical "sloothering slide of her" (*FW*, 195.03) to the Anna Livia chapter and the conclusion of Book I.

Joyce's own favorite, the Anna Livia chapter, while foreshadowing the ending of *Finnegans Wake* with its flowing and fading lyricism, gives voice to two washerwomen who gossip with each other about ALP and that "awful old reppe" (*FW*, 196.11). The gossip runs its expected course of inquiry and innuendo through the various stages of the relationship between HCE and ALP but also draws out Anna Livia's role as "old Moppa Necessity" (*FW*, 207.29). Though in her loyalty to HCE she appears "nearly as badher as him herself" (*FW*, 198.09), Anna Livia also sustains her "hundred and how" (*FW*, 201.34) children with a dazzling array of gifts, ranging from the most basic and practical to Nobel prizes for artists "to sweeden their bitters" (*FW*, 211.03). Since "every telling has a taling" (*FW*, 213.12), the first book of the *Wake* now fades into darkness as the washerwomen appear to turn into a tree and a stone, but their round of gossipy tales, in affirming ALP as life sustainer, indicates that the reader should prepare for a renewal of the inquiry: "Teems of times and happy returns. The seim anew. Ordovico or viricordo. Anna was, Livia is, Plurabelle's to be" (*FW*, 215.22–24).

Book II renews the inquiry, but its mode and direction now shift from the parents to the children. The four chapters, beginning with The Mime of Mick, Nick, and the Maggies, take the reader through a round of games, homework, stories, and commentaries that despite the growing complication and density reveals a world of childish jealousies, rivalries, and conflicts. In a letter to Harriet Weaver Joyce described the "scheme" of the ninth chapter as based on "the game we used to call Angels and Devils or colours. The Angels, girls, are grouped behind the Angel, Shawn, and the Devil has to come over three times and ask for a colour. If the colour he asks for has been chosen by any girl she has to run and he tries to catch her" (*Letters*, 1:295).

The *Wake* inquiry then moves on to a guessing game in which the children play out a miniature drama of childish teasing and rivalry, foreshadowing their initiation into the adult world of seduction and betrayal that seems to lie at the heart of the fall. In the Wakean version of Angels and Devils, the devilish Glugg, or Shem, tries and fails three times to guess the color of the girls' "brideness" (*FW*, 223.06), despite pointed hints from Issy that the answer is heliotrope. Each time Glugg fails the girls dance around angelic Chuff, or Shaun, while Glugg goes off to pout and threatens to write "a most moraculous jeeremyhead sindbook" (*FW*, 229.32) about the family. The game eventually leads to the inevitable clash between the brothers and the intervention of the parents—"Housefather calls enthreateningly" (*FW*, 246.06)—who summon the children to do their lessons.

The next chapter further reinforces the shift in the *Wake* to the child's mode of inquiry by allowing the reader to observe the children doing their lessons. Patrick McCarthy believes that what seems important at this point in the *Wake* is that "the children have begun to take over from their parents, whose lives and sins they reenact and discuss with relish."[16] The comment seems premature, however, since the children are still merely playful and mischievous. The best hope for the inquiry in this round is that "some progress" can be made "on stilts" (*FW*, 236.26), that the child's world even in its playfulness will reveal some truth or key needed to solve the book's guessing game.

The lessons chapter is one of the *Wake*'s most complex because of its technique, which Joyce described as "a reproduction of a schoolboy's (and schoolgirl's) old classbook complete with marginalia by the twins, who change sides at half time, footnotes by the girl (who doesn't), a Euclid diagram, funny drawings etc." (*Letters*, 1:406). As the children work their way through an impressive array of subjects from the arts and sciences, each has a commentary appropriate to his or her personality. Whereas Shaun offers pompous, Latinized commentary, Shem's comments vulgarize and subvert; Issy's footnotes in turn are flirtatious and distracting.

If ever the reader needed a multifocal lens for the *Wake* inquiry, it is for the lessons chapter, with its "triv and quad" (*FW*, 306.12–13) and its conflicting marginalia and irreverent footnotes. The lessons, however, no matter how often the subject changes, contain the familiar characters—"not a feature alike and the face the same" (*FW,* 263.16)—and incidents—"The tasks above are as the flasks below"— (*FW,* 263.21) of the *Wake.* In other words any subject of inquiry leads the reader inevitably to HCE and his fall—"O felicitous culpability, sweet bad cess to you for an archetypt" (*FW,* 263.30)—and the antics of ALP, or in this case the notorious Euclid diagram of "ann aquilittoral dryankle" (*FW,* 286.19–20). The diagram, a collaboration between a scheming Shem and a gullible Shaun—Dolph and Kev in this episode—turns out to be a scandalous drawing of "the whome of your eternal geomater" (*FW,* 296–97.31–01). While the act of drawing ALP's "umdescribables" contains a wonderful parody of Yeats's *A Vision,* especially the section on the passage of the soul between lives, the diagram itself becomes a prefiguration of the children's sexual awakening and, as their playful but ominous letter and signatures indicate, the beginning of the end of the parents' authority and control: "With our best youlldied greedings to Pep and Memmy and the old folkers below and beyant" (*FW,* 308.21–23).

The import of the Euclidean prefiguration becomes manifest in the storytelling of the next chapter, as the Wakean scene and its inquiry shift to the "old folkers below" and the story of Kersse the tailor and the Norwegian Captain, followed by the tale of How Buckley Shot the Russian General. The Wakean versions of the poor tailor's futile attempts to fit a suit of clothes to the misshapen captain and the soldier's reluctance to shoot because of the general's vulnerable position take on significance for the inquiry because of the cyclical telling of the stories and what the stories reveal about the coming-of-age of generations and their passing. The "long after once," thrice-told tale of "the toyler in the tawn" and the way he "buttonhaled the Norweeger's capstan" (*FW,* 311.05–09) is also an account of HCE as the perennial invader—"the bugganeering wanderducken" (*FW,* 323.01)—and the effort to fit the native culture to his demands while assimilating his foreign nature through marriage: "there's no pure rube like an ool pool roober" (*FW,* 328.01). Once, however, "the wild main from Borneholm has jest come to crown" (*FW,* 331.35–36), the "Twwinns" (*FW,* 330.30), splitting the personality of Buckley into Butt and Taff, conspire to overthrow the HCE figure, even though the "strength of the rawshorn generand is known throughout the world" (*FW,* 335.21–22). With Shemese Taff playing Cassius to Shaunian Butt, the twins overthrow the invading father for "beheaving up that sob of tunf for to claimhis" (*FW,* 353.16–17) and in effect cause the "abnihilisation of the etym" and the resulting chaos: "an invanmorinthorrorumblefragoromboassity amidwhiches general uttermosts confussion are perceivable" (FW, 353.22, 24–26).

That the listeners grasp the moral of the stories becomes evident in their conclusion that HCE "hade to die it" (FW, 358.36) and in their unruly, threatening behavior toward Earwicker as they leave the pub. That Earwicker gets the "jest" becomes apparent in his defensive behavior and in his general collapse once he is left alone: "the feels of the fumes in the wakes of his ears our wineman from Barleyhome he just slumped to thorne" (FW, 382.24–26). The reader, however, after "Andoring the games, induring the studies, undaring the stories" (FW, 368.34–35), has one more trip before coming to the "end all" (FW, 368.35) of Book II and its inquiry into the family.

The twelfth chapter closes Book II with a synoptic view of "Trustan with Usolde" (FW, 383.17). As the young lovers sail forth to a new round of Vichian cycles—"Tristy's the spry young spark / That'll tread her and wed her and bed and red her" (FW, 383.11–12)—they leave behind the fallen King Mark—"Sure he hasn't got much of a bark"— (FW, 383.02)—and the voyeuristic four old men, who fade out to the inevitable rewards of old age: "pass the teeth . . . by the world forgot . . . poor bedsores . . . gangrene spentacles" (FW, 397.24–35). As for the Wake inquiry, the reader's best and last hope lies with "the mose likable lad that's come my ways yet" (FW, 399.27), now that the new generation appears to be ready to replace the old: "the way is free. Their lot is cast" (FW, 399.33).

The four chapters of Book III prove the Vichian structure of Finnegans Wake by illustrating that the more the inquiry appears to move away from the fallen figure of HCE to the next generation, the more likely it is, in the looking-glass world of the Wake, that the reader will encounter HCE himself. In Book III, the road to HCE lies with and through Shaun the Post, but before the long-awaited climactic meeting, which occurs in the fifteenth chapter (the third in Book III), the reader must endure two chapters of beamish Shaun—"it is hardly too much to say that he was looking grand" (FW, 405.15–16)—and his claims on Shem and Issy. In the first chapter of Book III, despite a series of questions designed to probe for information on HCE and the letter, Shaun's answers lead to his obsession with his brother and the usual charges, draped at least partly in the fable of the Ondt and the Gracehoper, of libel, plagiarism, and insanity: "The lowquacity of him. . . . The last word in stolentelling" (FW, 424.34–35).

In the next chapter Shaun, now as "Jaunty Jaun" (*FW,* 429.01), appears to have started on his round, but he pauses at this point for a long sermon to Issy and her "goodwill girls" (*FW,* 430.19) to put them "on their best beehiviour" (*FW,* 430.19) until he returns to their chorus of praise and appreciation. His advice is that they "adhere to as many as probable of the ten commandments" (*FW,* 432.26–27), even if Shaun's commandments appear more Wakean than Mosaic: "First thou shalt not smile. Twice thou shalt not love. Lust, thou shalt not commix idolatry" (*FW,* 433.21–22). Shaun's sermon also contains pointed references to incidents relevant to the inquiry—"look before you leak, dears" (*FW,* 433.34)—handy advice for the *Wake* reader—"Skim over *Through Hell with the Papes* [mostly boys] by the divine comic Denti Alligator" (*FW,* 440.05–06)—and the expected warnings against his brother, though he is "leaving my darling proxy behind for your consolering, lost Dave the Dancekerl" (*FW,* 462.16–17). Finally, after nearly toppling over, Shaun returns to his "feat of passage" (*FW,* 473.15) with the assurance that his heroic "farfetched deed" (*FW,* 473.15) will bring light and a new day out of the night's gloom and doom: "Eftsoon so too will our sphoenix spark spirt his spyre and sunward stride the rampante flambe. Ay, already the sombrer opacities of the gloom are sphanished! Brave footsore Haun! Work your progress! Hold to! Now! Win out, ye divil ye! The silent cock shall crow at last. The west shall shake the east awake. Walk while ye have the night for morn, lightbreakfastbringer, morroweth whereon every past shall full fost sleep. Amain" (*FW,* 473.18–25).

Unfortunately, the promise of the second chapter of Book III seems dashed at the beginning of the next chapter. Jaunty Jaun, whose journey was apparently to be a "riverrun" (*FW,* 03.01) to the source or beginning of *Finnegans Wake,* lies barrel-wrecked as Pure Yawn. Jaun's boasts have turned out to be nothing more than Yawn's "dream monologue" (*FW,* 474.04) within the dream of the *Wake.* Yet Yawn's failure will soon emerge as a fortunate fall for the reader and the happiest of coincidences in Joyce's coincidence-riddled book because the Gulliver-like Yawn lies sprawled on the *Wake*'s "historical grouns. . . . This same prehistoric barrow" (*FW,* 477.35–36) that reportedly contains the remains of the letter and of HCE himself.

The Wakean inquiry, now a "starchamber quiry" (*FW,* 475.18–19) conducted mutually by the four old men as "mamalujo" (*FW,* 476.32), becomes a burrowing into the barrow, an "exagmination" (*FW,* 497.02) through layer after layer of enveloping facts and rumors about HCE,

ALP, and the family. The burrowing, after a moment of silence, also yields a remarkable account of HCE's history from his residence in the Garden of Eden—"This common or garden . . . the wellknown kikkin-midden where the illassorted first couple first met with each other" (*FW*, 503.08–09)—to his present fallen and divided state as "this old boy 'Tom' or 'Thim' " who "is not all there, and is all the more himself since he is not so" (*FW*, 507.01–04). This astounding discovery—"How culious an epiphany" (*FW*, 508.11)—that the reader is at the site of the original fall, which as it turns out in the Vichian whirl of the *Wake* is also where every other fall, either in ballad or at the pub in Chapelizod, has taken place, becomes prelude to the book's climactic moment: "All halt! Sponsor programme and close down. That's enough, genral of finicking about Finnegan and fiddling with his faddles" (*FW*, 531.27–28).

Responding at last to the inquiry's summons, HCE arises to address the reader, but his initial response to all the charges against him is disappointing. Surrounded by layers of artifacts and rumors, he still claims that he is "known throughout the world . . . as a cleanliving man" (*FW*, 532.10–14), that there is "not one teaspoonspill of evidence" (*FW*, 534.09–10), except for lies and libel: "I have lived true thousand hells" (*FW*, 535.28). His stutter gives him away, however, and after a plea for sympathy finally decides that he cannot let others bear his burdens any longer. Accepting responsibility for his sins and crimes, HCE now has his finest moment in the *Wake*. Taking on the burden of the fall, he now is in a position to claim credit for humanity's rise and accomplishments, which according to HCE are considerable and impressive. As a builder he has founded families and tribes, forged great cities and civilizations as well as the seven wonders of the world: "chopes pyramidous . . . and beaconphires and colosets" (*FW*, 553.10–11). As a father he has provided for his children, educated them, and established codes and laws for correct behavior: "did not I festfix with mortarboard my unniversiries. . . . pass through twelve Threadneedles (*FW*, 551.28, 33). Whether judged a qualified success or an ambitious failure, considering the decline or fall of most of his creations and constructions, HCE makes one last claim: that he has done it all, for better or for worse, for the world's "pleashadure" (*FW*, 554.07).

As Book III and the inquiry wind down, the sixteenth chapter seems to float close to the surface and consciousness as if in anticipation of the end of the dream—"Too mult sleepth" (*FW*, 555.01)—and the beginning of a new day. The chapter actually contains something resembling a plot as the parents, this time as "the very nice people" (*FW,* 560.23) Mr. and Mrs. Porter, are disturbed from their sleep by a cry from one of the children—Issy, Kevin, or Jerry. When the mother visits the children's rooms she discovers that Shemese Jerry was having a nightmare: "sonly all in your imagination" (*FW,* 565.29). After reassuring Jerry that there are "no panthares" or "bad bold faathern" (*FW,* 565.19–20) in the room, she returns to the aroused father and calms him down as "the dapplegray dawn drags nearing nigh for to wake all droners that drowse in Dublin" (*FW,* 585.20–21).

After the Vichian "Tiers, tiers and tiers" (*FW,* 590.30) of the first three books, Book IV brings an end to *Finnegans Wake* with a single chapter that begins with a call of "all downs to dayne. Array! Surrection!" (*FW,* 593.02–03) and closes with an invitation to return to the book's beginning: "The keys to. Given! A way a lone a last a loved a long the" (*FW,* 628.15–16). The chapter itself is a cheerful awakening to the promise of a new age: "sure, straight, slim, sturdy, serene, synthetical, swift" (*FW,* 596.32–33) and a return to normal conditions after "a long, very long, a dark, very dark, an allburt unend, scarce endurable, and we could add mostly quite various and somenwhat stumbletumbling night" (*FW,* 598.06–09). It also features an invocation to the "most venerable Kevin" (*FW,* 605.33–34); a brief reappearance of the comic Mute and Jute, this time as Muta and Juta; and a debate between the arch-druid and "Same Patholic" (*FW,* 611.10) over the true color of things, with the Berkeley-minded arch-druid arguing for an inner light, perceived prismatically as rainbow-colored, and patron-sainted Patholic claiming one true color, which, of course, turns out to be green.

Before, however, "the wholemole millwheeling vicociclometer" (*FW,* 614.27) begins another round of rounds that according to the debate will be the same but will appear anew, the book as the letter offers a "P.S." from ALP, who is "about fetted up with nonsery reams" (*FW,* 619.18). Her postscript, penned with soft and flowing lyricism, becomes a remarkable moment in *Finnegans Wake* because it views the book from a human perspective. After waking HCE and reminding him that she kept her bargain—"Your wish was mewill" (*FW,* 620.27)—and defended him—"you came safe through" (*FW,* 623.02–03)—ALP flows on, but to a "bitter ending" (*FW,* 627.35), because she sees the *Wake* through her own eyes and recognizes that something more human than a cycle is passing out: "It's something fails us. First we feel. Then we fall" (*FW,* 627.11). While the last chapter of *Finnegans Wake* anticipates and celebrates the dawning of a new age, ALP's postscript, in an old, "sad and weary" voice (*FW,* 628.01), asks only that the new generation and Joyce's readers "Bussoftlhee mememormee" (*FW,* 628.15–16).

Chapter Six
Joyce's Wake

Richard Ellmann begins his biography of Joyce by noting, "We are still learning to be James Joyce's contemporaries, to understand our interpreter" (Ellmann, 1). Ellmann's observation has interesting implications for Joyce's writing and for the writing about Joyce. Echoing Joyce's lament that nobody understood him, Ellmann draws attention to the continuing need to learn about Joyce's contemporaneity and to understand his interpretation of the modern world. The first task suggested by Ellmann's comment involves recognizing in the broadest sense the writers Joyce regarded as his contemporaries. While Joyce acknowledged, sometimes to their surprise, the influence of writers of his own age, he also believed he was the contemporary of writers of previous generations and ages. The second and perhaps more controversial task for Joyce readers involves understanding both Joyce's vision of the relationship between the word and the world and the critical interpretation of that vision. Joyce's intention of putting so many enigmas into his work that he would keep "the professors busy for centuries arguing over what I meant" has produced a world of words in itself of opinions, judgments, and theories that have influenced the reading and formed the reputation of Joyce. But according to Joyce, "that's the only way of insuring one's immortality" (Ellmann, 521).

Joyce's Contemporaries

Joyce's own recognition of the contemporaneity of his mission and vision to the masterworks and master writers of the past found expression in both the arrogance of the young man, flushed with his artistic potential, and the accomplishment of the mature artist, self-assured of his own genius. At the age of 19 Joyce, convinced of the universality and permanence of art, wrote to the 73-year old Ibsen that he had sounded his name defiantly, claimed for Ibsen his "rightful place in the history of the drama, . . . shown what as it seemed to me, was your highest excellence—your lofty impersonal power," and now greeted

him as kindred spirit "joyfully, with hope and with love" (*Letters*, 1:51–
52). In his youth and early career Joyce founded his own art upon the
rock of Aristotle's philosophy rather than the mysticism and revivalism
of his Irish contemporaries. On 8 February 1903 he wrote from Paris to
his brother Stanislaus, "[U]p to my eyes in Aristotle's Psychology. . . .
[D]amn vegetable verse and double damn vegetable philosophy" (*Letters*, 2:28). In his broadside "The Holy Office" Joyce claimed kinship
with "The mind of witty Aristotle" and warned that other poets would
"receive now from my lip / Peripatetic scholarship" (*CW*, 150).

Armed with aesthetic notebooks filled with paraphrases from Aristotle, Joyce constructed "in unchallengeable thereness" the physical
world of his fiction, beginning with the scrupulosity of his portraitures
in *Dubliners*.[1] In Aristotle's definition of the soul as the form of forms
he found justification for his designation of Stephen Dedalus as the
artist, and with Aristotle's principle of contradiction he founded the
narrative movement and form of *A Portrait of the Artist as a Young Man*.[2]
In *Ulysses* Stephen, who in *A Portrait* uses Aristotelian thought to
develop a theory of aesthetic apprehension, turns to Aristotle at critical
moments in the "Proteus" and "Scylla and Charybdis" episodes. Faced
with a whirling flux of contrary ideas and opposed attitudes, he uses
Aristotle to pin down the ineluctable character of the world around him
and to bring definition and order to his world within. Even in *Finnegans
Wake* Aristotle's ideas, though as grotesquely distorted as the language
and form of the *Wake* itself, still offer the reader some explanation of
how the book as letter got into its present condition.

With Aristotle for intellectual support Joyce found suitable companions in literature for his imaginative enterprises. Though he recognized
and borrowed ideas from the literature of his own contemporaries, he
found justification for his artistic mission primarily in the works of the
great artists of the past. Homer, Dante, and Shakespeare—described
by Mary Reynolds as "the dominant triad in *Ulysses*"[3]—were for Joyce
the old fathers, the old artificers, who stood him "now and ever in good
stead" (*P*, 253). Each had accomplished what Stephen Dedalus in *A
Portrait* sets as his lofty goal: "to forge in the smithy of my soul the
uncreated conscience of my race" (*P*, 253). Beyond providing narrative
scaffold or intellectual fodder for aesthetic debate, their works validated
the artist's authority and power to construct a world so vivid, compelling, and comprehensive that the reader encounters not only the reality
of experience but a vision of reality both universal and humane.

Joyce's own accomplishment in forging a new reality out of the materials of his art has manifested itself in the efforts of modern artists and critics to find suitable companions for Joyce in his own age. Typical is William York Tindall's declaration that Joyce, who "seems to have understood everything," created a vision of reality "almost as pervasive as that of Einstein or Freud."[4] Unlike Eliot, Pound, and Yeats, Joyce is often regarded as more ultramodern than modern.[5] His work, rather than expressing the conditions of his age as Eliot's *The Waste Land* does, appears to advance its intellectual borders. The world of Joyce's art, while containing Leopold Bloom and even the ubiquitous yet elusive HCE, rivals the theories of Einstein and Freud with its own multiple dimensions and murky depths. The forms of Joyce's art, while never failing to invite the reader, also invite comparisons with the complex perspectives and tonal effects of Picasso and Stravinsky.

To describe Joyce as the Einstein of literature can, however, be misleading because many of his interests and concerns were topical and common to the modern writer. Even though his expression of reality often appears to exceed even the most experimental forms of modern literature and to exasperate even the most sophisticated of modern readers, Joyce was only one of several major writers who attempted to reconcile the uncertain temporality of their age with the artistic quest for permanence—a task tantamount to finding resolution or creating harmony out of the conflict between Shem and Shaun. Thomas Mann, for example, saw Western civilization, caught up in the flux and mutability of modern life, as tottering on the brink of rage, chaos, and destruction. The uncertainty of Hans Castorp's fate in *The Magic Mountain* raises the question of whether or not art, culture, and society can even survive in a world gone mad.

Many twentieth-century writers, including Joyce, struggled to forge timeless images and to create a unifying vision out of a world apparently declining into the state of disorder, collapse, and violence so vividly described by Yeats in "The Second Coming":

> Things fall apart; the centre cannot hold
> Mere anarchy is loosed upon the world,
> The blood-dimmed tide is loosed, and everywhere
> The ceremony of innocence is drowned;
> The best lack all conviction, while the worst
> Are full of passionate intensity.

Some modern writers, like Marcel Proust, disturbed by a world of collapsing traditions and lost values, turned to personal memory for comfort and even salvation. Proust's art travels back in time so that memory can discover some moment in the past, such as the celebrated episode of the madeleine in *Swann's Way,* that restores deep feeling to the Proust hero. Other writers, like Virginia Woolf, finding no aesthetic grace in the personal past, create imaginative pleasure domes out of deeply felt or experienced moments. Woolf's characters, such as Mrs. Dalloway and Mrs. Ramsey, create intimate moments within dinner parties or seaside excursions that if arranged properly have the potential for becoming emotionally significant. Whereas Proust's hero searches in the past for deeply felt experiences, Woolf's heroines brave the present in the hope of creating halos of good feeling that will radiate throughout their lives and beyond.

Joyce's own art is as obsessed as Proust's with the past and records its own moments of epiphany out of the actual experiences of its characters. Yet for Joyce's characters the past is often the nightmare from which they are trying to escape, and the present, rendered in painstaking detail by Joyce, yields epiphanies that often expose emotional and moral failure. Unlike that of Proust or Woolf, Joyce's vision, rather than searching backward or escaping forward, found its correspondence in the same circularity that fascinated Mann, Eliot, and Yeats. In *The Magic Mountain* Mann's tuberculous hero, becoming lost in a snowstorm, discovers that his natural or instinctive moment is circular, though his discovery brings little comfort because it does not reveal whether circularity signifies renewal or merely endless repetition—"the seim anew." Later in the novel Mann does provide an answer when Castorp decides that the threads of a gramophone record signify the possibility of choice, within life's circular movement, between the spirals of life and death.

In Eliot's *The Waste Land* the gramophone record offers no more than a momentary distraction from an evening's unpleasantness, but the circular movement of events, the limbo world of *The Waste Land,* creates the opportunity for Eliot in the *Four Quartets* to find the still point of the wheel, the timeless moment in which the soul contemplates its own image in the eyes of God. Yeats, on the other hand, created in *A Vision* his own "Great Wheel," based on the 28 phases of the moon, and saw humanity and history spinning between the strength of the individual intellect and creative imagination and the demands of duty and morality. In his art, however, Yeats forged images to celebrate the triumphant joy of life and to challenge the mere anarchy of his own time.

While Joyce also forged images of circularity out of the material of his art, he found no comfort or solution to modern perplexities and anxieties in spirals, wheels, or circles. Instead, these patterns merely gave Joyce the dimensions for a verbal universe that through its own whirling language and laughter invites the reader to share in the joke, to see the extent of the human comedy no matter what the song, phase, or cycle. In *Ulysses* Joyce takes the spiraling gramophone record, given so much serious signification in *The Magic Mountain,* and transforms it, through Bloom's speculations in the "Hades" episode, into its comic counterpart: "Besides how could you remember everybody? Eyes, walk, voice. Well, the voice, yes: gramophone. Have a gramophone in every grave or keep it in the house. After dinner on a Sunday. Put on poor old greatgrandfather. Kraahraak! Hellohellohello amawfullyglad kraark awfullygladaseeragain hellohello amarawf kopthsth" (*U,* 93). In *Finnegans Wake* Joyce pokes fun at the high seriousness of Eliot and Yeats with occasional parodies of *The Waste Land* and *A Vision.* Yeats becomes especially vulnerable in the lessons chapter of the *Wake* when the Euclid diagram is admired with Yeatsian hyperbole—"One recalls Byzantium" (*FW,* 294.27)—is interpreted by the Yeatsian states of the soul in judgment—"When I'm dreaming back like that I begins to see" (*FW,* 295.10–11)—and is finally revealed, once the circles are drawn, as a sexual joke dressed up in Yeatsian imagery—"Gyre O, gyre O, gyrotundo" (*FW,* 295.23–24).

Joyce's own vision certainly has its serious dimensions, apparent in the limbo state of his Dubliners, the lofty aspirations of his artist, the arduous odyssey of his modern-day Ulysses, and the cosmic clashes of HCE and the family. Yet Joyce preferred an expression of wit and laughter to a display of Yeats's "right mastery." He delighted in subversive strategies rather than images of control. Rather than raging against humanity's few virtues and many follies, its seductive curves and unfortunate blemishes, Joyce found the human condition ineluctable, but as much the jester as the Aristotelian, he created his own labyrinth of puns and tricks out of the mutability of experience and the anxieties of his age.

As a realist Joyce recorded with "scrupulous meanness" the frustrations, disappointments, failings, and fallings of his characters. Even the enduring and enfolding ALP bitterly complains about her life—"A hundred cares, a tithe of troubles" (*FW,* 627.14)—and her family—"all me life I have been lived among them but now they are becoming lothed to me" (*FW,* 627.16–17). Yet as artist Joyce forged out of the richness of language and his imagination a fiction that delights in its own laughter, views the world as a profane comedy rather than a profound tragedy, and invites the reader to share in a joke while time and the age rage on. For Joyce there was no ignoring, defying, or beating time, as the Gracehoper reminds the Ondt in *Finnegans Wake*. No search for things past, no halo, spiral, or wheel could stay time's inevitable course. Instead, Joyce used words to take advantage of time, his age, and the reader. His literary gifts, while rendering life's actualities, also taught his age the lesson Shaun learned from his artist-brother Shem: "In the beginning was the gest he jousstly says" (*FW*, 468.05). For Joyce the creation of the first "gest" or word out of life's joust at the same time provoked the first jest and the coincidental laughter needed to counter human conflict. Joyce's art, then, becomes the embellishment of the first word and the original joke and his vision the happy coincidence of the radiating laughter of his readers.

Joyce's Followers

In his lifetime Joyce had many friends and associates willing to serve as disciples of his work. Though perhaps only Harriet Weaver merits sainthood in the Joycean canon, others—like Frank Budgen, Sylvia Beach, Stuart Gilbert, Herbert Gorman, Eugene and Maria Jolas, Ezra Pound, and the remaining apostles, especially Samuel Beckett, of *Our Exagmination Round his Factification for Incamination of Work in Progress*—deserve consideration for privileged status because of the special tasks they performed for Joyce. Still others, like Édourard Dujardin, James Stephens, and Ettore Schmitz (who wrote under the pseudonym Italo Svevo), received special recognition from Joyce himself, though each found the honor either undeserved or incomprehensible.

Joyce's work has in turn spawned its own followers, some among Joyce's own generation and many from later generations of artists and critics. T. S. Eliot, for example, may have believed that *Ulysses* made all past forms of the novel obsolete and closed down the novel's future, but the facsimile and transcript of the original drafts of *The Waste Land* show that Eliot's own borrowings from *Ulysses* were so obvious that Ezra Pound, reminded of Joyce, wrote "J. J." in the margin at one point and, in crossing out the word *yes* after a line from the "Game of Chess" section, wrote "Penelope/J. J."[6]

In *AfterJoyce* Robert Martin Adams states that "Joyce did not sound the death-knell of the novel, as he was once said to have done; he was not the sterile if splendid termination of a development, but a fecund and various influence on developing talents of many diverse sorts."[7] How fecund the influence and how diverse the talent are well detailed in the works of Breon Mitchell and Vivian Mercier, who have brought critical attention to Joyce's influence on the German novel and on the French *nouveau roman*.[8] Adams has in turn found Joyce's influence in the writings of novelists as diverse in nationality and vision as Virginia Woolf, William Faulkner, Samuel Beckett, Carlo Emilio Gadda, Vladimir Nabokov, Flann O'Brien, and Jorge Luis Borges.

While Joyce's fiction has influenced generations of writers, the reactions to Joyce have been as varied as the backgrounds of the writers themselves. Beckett, for example, though a devoted disciple of Joyce, created a literature of closed rather than comic possibilities and of isolated rather expansive personalities. Instead of Joyce's art of embellishment, Beckett, as if yielding to Joyce's mastery, preferred a language of limitation and found the conditions of entropy and silence more compatible to his vision than Joycean cycles and contraries. Flann O'Brien, on the other hand, found it so easy to accommodate his fiction to Joyce's influence that Joyce actually makes an appearance in O'Brien's *The Dalkey Archive*. O'Brien, however, turns biography into parody, as he reinvents a Joyce who wants to join the Jesuits; who denies having written *Ulysses*, which he regards as piece of filth; and who has never heard of *Finnegans Wake*, though he knows the ballad. In *At-Swim-Two-Birds*, a novel admired by Joyce, O'Brien carries the whole business of aesthetic and critical posturing to the point of complete absurdity by offering his own counteraesthetic. He claims that novels should not pretend to be anything more than shams and that a good novel, by plagiarizing other works, should offer the reader a chance to have a good time at someone else's expense, even if the joke is on the grand jester, Joyce himself.

While O'Brien tried to outwit rather than submit to his fellow Irishman, American writers, neither mocking nor surrendering to Joyce, have found his writing and vision so relevant to their own fictions that they have readily borrowed Joycean ideas and techniques. William Faulkner, the foremost American novelist influenced by Joyce, exploited Joyce in early writings like *Mosquitoes* and the short story "Artist at Home" as part of his ridicule and rejection of Sherwood Anderson, who greatly admired and championed Joyce's work. Once free of Anderson's influence, however, Faulkner returned to Joyce, though he often claimed he had never read Joyce's writing. Faulkner's major works, beginning with *Sartoris* and *The Sound and the Fury*, display obvious parallels with Joyce's fiction in characterization, theme, and experimental technique. Other American novelists and dramatists, borrowing heavily from *A Portrait of the Artist as a Young Man, Ulysses*, and *Finnegans Wake*, have also produced strikingly experimental works, most notably Ralph Ellison's *Invisible Man*, Thornton Wilder's *The Skin of Our Teeth*, and William Gass's *Omensetter's Luck*, as well as the novels of metafictionists like John Barth and Thomas Pynchon.

While Joyce's fiction has been a rich sourcebook for generations of European and American artists, his life and writing have been equally hospitable to decades of critical cycles and conflicts. As early as 1927 Joyce approached Stuart Gilbert with the idea of an authorized biography but finally decided on Herbert Gorman, but with the stipulation to Gorman that the biography would not be published without Joyce's approval of the entire text. In fact Joyce took great pains with the typescript and proofs to ensure that the biography recorded his personal ordeals and self-styled martyrdom to his art and indicted those who had betrayed him. While Richard Ellmann had only the ghost of Joyce looking over his shoulder, his later, far more comprehensive and distinguished biography still echoes its precursor's characterizations, which Ellmann greatly enhanced by injecting Joyce's fiction into the mainstream of the biography itself.

Just as Joyce arranged his biography to suit his artistic vision and re-created his life through his fiction, he also provided early critical approaches to his work, out of either the anger of rejection or the perception that his readers would need encouragement and guidance, especially in navigating their way through *Ulysses* and *Finnegans Wake*. His pronouncements on *Dubliners* and his commentary on *Chamber Music, A Portrait*, and *Exiles* are now embedded in the critical landscape. His letters explaining his works in progress are now firmly fixed in critical notes and annotations. He also chaperoned the early criticism of *Ulysses* and arranged for an apostolic reading of *Finnegans Wake*.

While following Joyce's leads, his critics have also developed their own paths through the labyrinthine world of his fiction. Their critical burrowings and landscaping have produced impressive readings and explications, as well as intricate historical and theoretical designs, that have revealed Joyce as an inviting host for inquiry and comparison and his work as rich in critical and theoretical possibilities. Though Joyce declared himself an Aristotelian, resisted psychoanalysis, and appeared detached from politics, his critics have found his work compatible with

Bergsonian streams, Freudian complexes, Jungian archetypes, and Marxian ideology.[9] While Joyce's works draw attention to Homer, Dante, and Shakespeare as the cultural authorities of his own artistic vision, Joyce's critics have discovered rich veins of popular literature and culture in the body of his fiction.[10] The creator of the artist in rebellion, the bourgeois Ulysses, and the earth-mother Molly, Joyce has, by contrast, been judged thoroughly Irish in character, resistant to paternal or authoritarian social structures, and responsive to feminist issues and concerns.[11] The builder of symbolic structures, epic scaffolds, and universal cycles, he is also credited with devising a literature so subversive in its language that it undermines conventional assumptions about and claims for the authority of character and theme, destabilizes the legitimacy of the critical search for meaning, and reduces all inquires to studies of the text as self-reflective and self-referential.[12]

In the past several decades, then, critics, while following in the wake of Joyce's fiction, have created their own fictions; woven their own figures, patterns, and cycles; and challenged and even sometimes dismissed those perceived as assuming authority or propriety over Joyce's world. The critical discussion of Joyce since his death in 1941, while impressive in its intensity and complexity, has also become so massive in its outpouring that Joyce studies are now commonly referred to as the "Joyce Industry." Not surprisingly, the institutionalizing of the study of Joyce has generated its own history—its pioneers mapping out the territory, its critical moments and movements, its identification of generations of scholars and even ages of criticism, and its sense of being both at the center of modernist thinking and the cutting edge of postmodern theory.

The rise of a Joyce establishment does not, however, appear to have caused restrictiveness or rigidity in Joyce scholarship. As Benstock points out, "Each generation redefines the set of Joycean problems and every Joyce text—not only the inexhaustible *Ulysses* and *Finnegans Wake*—reactivates critical responses and approaches. For every critic who has attempted to nail shut a particular area of consideration, dozens immediately appear with crowbars to pull up the floor boards." Benstock does, however, add that "a community—or several interrelated communities—has emerged during the past two decades, to share problems and pool resources, a communal effort that has made the work of each of us much easier and lessened the possibility of certain errors that take root in isolation" (Benstock, 1–2).

This sense of community has allowed Joyce studies to develop a clear

sense of Joyce's place in modern literature and his role in defining modernity, while at the same time opening up Joyce scholarship to the most
radical thinking in postmodern literary criticism. Joyce's critics have
traced his early fiction to the European roots of modernism, especially to
the writings of Maupassant, Flaubert, and the French symbolists, while
keeping a constant focus on Joyce's Irish Catholic background and Jesuit
training. They have also established Joyce's imposing credentials as an
innovator by recognizing his remarkable advancement of the novel to
newer and newer forms, his radical experiments with style and structure,
and his ever-expanding vision of the possibilities of language no matter
how familiar and redundant the human condition and experience. Recent Joyce studies see his foregrounding and free play with language as
self-apparent and self-sustaining, while subverting all other critical
claims to Joyce's intentions in his art.

Yet out of all the energizing conflicts and controversies, the passing
and gathering of generations of writers and critics, Joyce studies are
still founded upon a critical world that Joyce anticipated and cultivated. Those who enter that world then become part of the "funferal" of
Joyce's fiction, with its multiple puns, radiating laughter, and comic
vision. Critics will no doubt continue the serious debate on whether
Joyce's laughter is expansive or reductive, hopeful or cynical, but Joyce,
the teller and often the object of the tale, apparently concerned himself
with developing the reader's capacity for finding the joke and delight-
ing in the laughter. Though complex and demanding, Joyce's world
remains rich in comic possibilities and still invites the reader to journey
through one of the most remarkable verbal labyrinths and imaginative
odysseys ever devised by the artist.

Notes and References

Chapter One

1. For the historical context of the year of Joyce's birth, see Bernard Benstock, *James Joyce* (New York: Unger, 1985), 2–6; hereafter cited in text.

2. For a detailed account of the Joyce family, see Richard Ellmann, *James Joyce* (New York: Oxford University Press, 1982), 11–22; hereafter cited in text.

3. *A Portrait of the Artist as a Young Man* (New York: Viking Press, 1964), 65; hereafter cited in text as *P*.

4. The poem so pleased John Joyce that he had copies printed and distributed to his friends; see Ellmann, 33–34.

5. *The Critical Writings of James Joyce*, ed. Ellsworth Mason and Richard Ellmann (New York: Viking Press, 1959), 228; hereafter cited in text as *CW*.

6. *Ulysses* (New York: Random House, 1986), 34; hereafter cited in text as *U*.

7. *Stephen Hero* (New York: New Directions, 1963), 211; hereafter cited in text as *SH*.

8. *Letters of James Joyce*, 3 vols., ed. Stuart Gilbert (vol. 1) and Richard Ellmann (vols. 2–3) (New York: Viking Press, 1966), 2:28–29; hereafter cited in text as *Letters*.

9. For a full account of Nora Barnacle's life, see Brenda Maddox, *Nora: The Real Life of Molly Bloom* (Boston: Houghton Mifflin, 1988).

10. For an account of the circumstances of this incident, see Ellmann, 184.

11. See Ellmann, 270–72; see also *James Joyce: The Critical Heritage*, ed. Robert H. Deming (New York: Barnes and Noble, 1970), 1:36–42.

12. For the correspondence between Joyce and Nora during this period, see *Letters*, 2:230–82; see also *Selected Letters of James Joyce*, ed. Richard Ellmann (New York: Viking Press, 1975), 157–96.

13. Pound also arranged for the publication of "A Curious History," on the earlier rejection of *Dubliners*, in an issue of the *Egoist* preceding the serialization of *A Portrait*.

14. Stanislaus Joyce, unfortunately, was arrested in June 1915 and spent the remainder of the war in Austrian detention camps.

15. The episodes brought the novel through the morning hours with Bloom to "Aeolus."

16. The confiscated issues contained the "Lestrygonians," "Scylla and Charybdis," "Nausicaa," and "Cyclops" episodes.

17. See Deming, 1:191–239.

18. The pages—a sketch of King Roderick O'Conor of Ireland—in an embellished form eventually became part of the third chapter of Book II of *Finnegans Wake*.

19. Among those signing the protest were Albert Einstein, Bertrand Russell, D. H. Lawrence, Thomas Mann, and William Butler Yeats. George Bernard Shaw and Ezra Pound, however, refused to add their names.

20. Among the 12 contributors were Frank Budgen, Stuart Gilbert, Eugene Jolas, William Carlos Williams, and Samuel Beckett.

21. See Ellmann, 722–23.

22. See Maddox, 346–401.

23. See Maddox, 362–63.

24. Trilling, *Commentary* 45 (February 1968): 53.

25. Burgess, *Spectator,* 2 December 1966, 726.

26. Howe, *New York Times Book Review,* 23 November 1975, 3.

Chapter Two

1. *The Letters of Ezra Pound,* ed. D. D. Paige (New York: Harcourt Brace, 1950), 153.

2. Robert Scholes and Richard Kain, eds., *The Workshop of Daedalus: James Joyce and the Raw Material for "A Portrait of the Artist as a Young Man"* (Evanston, Ill.: Northwestern University Press, 1965), 6–7; hereafter cited in text.

3. *Chamber Music,* ed. William York Tindall (New York: Columbia University Press, 1954), 3; hereafter cited in text as *CM.*

4. For Joyce's note of explanation, see Ellmann, 262. For a discussion of *Chamber Music* based on Joyce's explanation, see Robert Boyle, "The Woman Hidden in Joyce's *Chamber Music,*" in *Women in Joyce,* ed. Suzette Henke and Elaine Unkeless (Urbana: University of Illinois Press, 1982), 3–30.

5. See Ellmann, 360–61.

6. Florence Walzl, *"Dubliners,"* in *A Companion to Joyce Studies,* ed. Zack Bowen and James F. Carens (Westport, Conn.: Greenwood Press, 1984), 157.

7. *Selected Letters,* trans. Francis Steegmuller (New York: Farrar, Straus, and Giroux, 1954), 195.

8. Morris Beja, "Epiphany and Epiphanies," in *A Companion to Joyce Studies,* 716.

9. *Dubliners* (New York: Viking Press, 1967), 171; hereafter cited in text as *D.*

10. Phillip F. Herring sees *gnomon, paralysis,* and *simony* as three key words, not just in the first story but in formulating an uncertainty principle in *Dubliners* in general; see Phillip F. Herring, *Joyce's Uncertainty Principle* (Princeton, N.J.: Princeton University Press, 1987), x, 3–8, 10–14.

11. Joyce critics who read *Dubliners* on a symbolic level see the Pigeon

House as part of a matrix of religious images in the stories; see, for example, Brewster Ghiselin, "The Unity of Joyce's *Dubliners,*" *Accent* 16 (Spring 1956): 75–88. Later critics have read the story more in terms of the "queer old josser" as the first in a series of oppressive, perverse father figures; see, for example, Frances L. Restuccia, *Joyce and the Law of the Father* (New Haven, Conn.: Yale University Press, 1989), 3–4.

12. See, for example, Bernard Benstock, "Arabesques: Third Position of Concord," *James Joyce Quarterly* 5 (Fall 1967): 30–39.

13. Craig Hansen Werner, however, gives the story credibility by linking Jimmy Doyle with Eveline as victims of social and religious structures; see Craig Hansen Werner, *Dubliners: A Pluralistic World* (Boston: Twayne Publishers, 1988), 36–38.

14. Joyce's critics tend to see his portraits of women as painfully and scrupulously honest in their revelation of women's oppressive conditions in Irish society; see, for example, Margot Norris, "Narration under a Blindfold: Reading Joyce's 'Clay' " in *PMLA* 102 (March 1987): 206–15.

Chapter Three

1. "A Portrait of the Artist," in *A Portrait of the Artist as a Young Man: Text, Criticism, and Notes,* ed. Chester G. Anderson (New York: Viking Press, 1968), 258–66.

2. Thomas Connolly, "Stephen Hero," in *Companion to Joyce Studies,* 229.

3. Ezra Pound, 15 September letter to Joyce, in *Text, Criticism, and Notes,* 318; hereafter cited in text.

4. See, for example, William York Tindall's *A Reader's Guide to James Joyce* (New York: Noonday Press, 1959), 86–93, as opposed to Bernard Benstock's *James Joyce* (New York: Ungar, 1985), 52–53.

5. For an excellent summary, see Thomas F. Staley, "Strings with the Labyrinth: Sixty Years with Joyce's *Portrait,*" in *Approaches to Joyce's "Portrait,"* ed. Thomas F. Staley and Bernard Benstock (Pittsburgh: University of Pittsburgh Press, 1976), 3–24. See also Staley's "James Joyce," in *Anglo-Irish Literature: A Review of Research,* ed. Richard J. Finneran (New York: Modern Language Association of America, 1976), 402–10.

6. See Anderson, "Editor's Introduction," in *Text, Criticism, and Notes,* 446–54.

7. See Hugh Kenner, "The Cubist *Portrait,*" in *Approaches to Joyce's "Portrait,"* 177–84; see also Kenner "The '*Portrait*' in Perspective," in *Text, Criticism, and Notes,* 426, 439.

8. Edmund Epstein dates the section "about October ninth or tenth, 1891" and believes Stephen's dream would be occurring at the same time that "Parnell's body was brought to Ireland on October, 11, 1891." He also shows how Joyce "distorts both fictional and real chronology to effect a coincidence of little Stephen's rebellion and the death of Parnell." See Edmund Epstein, *The*

Ordeal of Stephen Dedalus (Carbondale: Southern Illinois University Press, 1971), 36–37. For an attempt at a physical time scheme, see appendix A in Robert M. Adams, *James Joyce: Common Sense and Beyond* (New York: Random House, 1966), 217–20.

9. For an expanded view, see Richard F. Peterson, "Stephen and the Narrative of *A Portrait of the Artist as a Young Man*," in *Work in Progress: Joyce Centenary Essays*, ed. Richard F. Peterson, Alan M. Cohn, and Edmund L. Epstein (Carbondale: Southern Illinois University Press, 1983), 15–29. John Paul Riquelme sees these narrative changes as acts more of displacement than of continuity; see John Paul Riquelme, *Teller and Tale in Joyce's Fiction* (Baltimore: John Hopkins University Press, 1983), 48–85.

10. For an excellent discussion of Stephen's theory, see S. L. Goldberg's chapter, in *The Classical Temper* (London: Chatto and Windus, 1961), 41–65.

Chapter Four

1. See Ellmann, 355–56.

2. *Exiles* (New York: Penguin, 1973), 71; hereafter cited in text as *E*.

3. Bernard Benstock, "*Exiles*," in *A Companion to Joyce Studies*, 362–63, 376.

4. For a discussion of the backgrounds of *Exiles*, see John MacNicholas, *James Joyce's "Exiles": A Textual Companion* (New York: Garland Publishing, 1979), 5–16.

5. See Ellmann, 527–28.

6. See Ellmann, 443, 528, 530–31.

7. Richard Kain, *Fabulous Voyager: A Study of James Joyce's "Ulysses"* (New York: Viking Press, 1959), 98–99.

8. Frank Budgen, *James Joyce and the Making of "Ulysses"* (Bloomington: Indiana University Press, 1960), 59; hereafter cited in text.

9. See, for example, Zack Bowen, "*Ulysses*," in *A Companion to Joyce Studies*, 548–49; hereafter cited in text.

10. Stuart Gilbert, *James Joyce's "Ulysses"* (New York: Vintage Books, 1952), 10; hereafter cited in text.

11. For an early, thorough study of Homeric correspondences, see Gilbert. For a later study of the epic patterns and relationships between Homer and Joyce, see Michael Seidel, *Epic Geography: James Joyce's "Ulysses"* (Princeton, N.J.: Princeton University Press, 1976).

12. A. Walton Litz, *James Joyce* (New York: Twayne Publishers, 1966), 117.

13. Ezra Pound, "Pound on *Ulysses* and Flaubert," in *The Critical Heritage*, 266.

14. T. S. Eliot, "*Ulysses*, Order, and Myth," in *James Joyce: Two Decades of Criticism* (New York: Vanguard Press, 1948), 201.

15. Karen Lawrence, *The Odyssey of Style in "Ulysses"* (Princeton, N.J.: Princeton University Press, 1981), 2.

16. For a critical summary, see Hugh Kenner, "Critical Sequels," in *Ulysses* (Baltimore: Johns Hopkins University Press, 1987), 169–73; hereafter cited in text. Kenner has been effective in publicizing the idea of the Arranger, which in actuality was originated by David Hayman in *"Ulysses": The Mechanics of Meaning* (Madison: University of Wisconsin Press, 1982), 88–104. For a summary of the debate on the Arranger and other narrative principles, see Patrick McGee, *Paperspace: Style as Ideology in Joyce's "Ulysses"* (Lincoln: University of Nebraska Press, 1988), 214–15; McGee in turn argues for an Arranger and Deranger, 72–85.

17. See the summary in Patrick A. McCarthy, *"Ulysses": Portals of Discovery* (Boston: Twayne Publishers, 1990), 21–22. See also Michael Patrick Gillespie's comment in *Reading the Book of Himself: Narrative Strategies in the Works of Joyce* (Columbus: Ohio State University Press, 1989) that "with the composition of *Ulysses* Joyce moves his aesthetic and artistic allegiances from Modernism to Postmodernism" (173). For a view that balances Joyce's words with the reader's world, see Marilyn French, *The Book as World: James Joyce's "Ulysses"* (Cambridge, Mass.: Harvard University Press, 1976).

18. C. H. Peake, *James Joyce: The Citizen and the Artist* (Stanford, Calif.: Stanford University Press, 1977), 111; hereafter cited in text.

19. For an expanded discussion, see Richard F. Peterson, "Did Joyce Write *Hamlet?*," *James Joyce Quarterly* 27 (Winter 1980): 365–71. See also S. L. Goldberg, *The Classical Temper*, 66–99.

20. See, for example, Lawrence, 80.

21. See Joseph Frank, "Spatial Form in Modern Literature," (revision of the original version published in *Sewanee Review* in 1945), in *The Widening Gyre: Crisis in Mastery in Modern Literature* (Bloomington: Indiana University Press, 1963), 3–62, in contrast to Kain, 45.

22. See Bowen, 92.

23. For a discussion of the "realistic comic philosophy" of *Ulysses* and the roots of that philosophy in comic traditions, see Zack Bowen, *Ulysses as a Comic Novel* (Syracuse, N.Y.: Syracuse University Press, 1989).

Chapter Five

1. The text of the ballad appears in a number of critical works. See, for example, Ellmann, 557, or Roland McHugh, *Annotations to "Finnegans Wake"* (Baltimore: Johns Hopkins University Press, 1980), 4, 6, 15, 24.

2. *Finnegans Wake* (New York: Viking Press, 1939), 4.18; hereafter cited in text as *FW*.

3. Mary Colum and Padraic Colum, *Our Friend James Joyce* (Garden City, N.Y.: Doubleday, 1958), 123.

4. Clive Hart, *Structure and Motif in "Finnegans Wake"* (Evanston, Ill.: Northwestern University Press, 1962), 50.

5. Joseph Campbell and Henry Morton Robinson, *A Skeleton Key to "Finnegans Wake"* (New York: Harcourt Brace, 1944). For a summary of efforts to give titles to the chapters of *Wake,* see Bernard Benstock, *Joyce-again's Wake: An Analysis of "Finnegans Wake"* (Seattle: University of Washington Press, 1965), 5–6.

6. For a recent discussion of the important relationship between Vico and *Finnegans Wake,* see John Bishop, *Joyce's Book of the Dark* (Madison: University of Wisconsin Press, 1986), 174–215. See also Donald Phillip Verene, ed., *Vico and Joyce* (Albany: State University of New York Press, 1986), 59–131.

7. For a recent discussion, see Theoharis Constantine Theoharis, *Joyce's "Ulysses": An Anatomy of the Soul* (Chapel Hill: University of North Carolina Press, 1988), 39–87. For a discussion of Joyce's chapters in *Ulysses* as defined by opposing extremes, see James H. Maddox, Jr., *Joyce's "Ulysses" and the Assault upon Character* (New Brunswick, N.J.: Rutgers Press, 1978). For Bruno and the *Wake,* see, for example, James S. Atherton, *The Books at the Wake* (Carbondale: Southern Illinois University Press, 1974), 36–37; for Atherton on Vico, see 29–34.

8. For an approach to *Finnegans Wake* based on Joyce's use of sigla, see Roland McHugh, *The Sigla of "Finnegans Wake"* (Austin: University of Texas Press, 1976).

9. See McHugh.

10. See, for example, the chapter on "The Identity of the Dreamer" in Bishop, 126–45.

11. This opening riddle of the letter chapter does, of course, play upon the first riddle—guessing the title of his work in progress—that Joyce posed to the early and often-reluctant reader of *Wake.*

12. For a discussion of the Wakean concern for the letter, see, for example, Benstock's *James Joyce,* 169–74.

13. Thomas Staley has rounded off Joyce studies into the "Age of Criticism" and the "Age of Theory"; see Thomas Staley, "James Joyce," in *Recent Research on Anglo-Irish Writers,* ed. Richard J. Finneran (New York: Modern Language Association of America, 1983), 181.

14. For critical barometers of the changes in *Wake* studies and Joyce studies in general, see the various collections of essays from International Joyce symposia. For a recent assessment, see the introduction to Morris Beja and Shari Benstock, eds., *Coping with Joyce: Essays from the Copenhagen Symposium* (Columbus: Ohio State University Press, 1989), ix–xv.

15. See, for example, Clive Hart, "Afterword: Reading *Finnegans Wake,*" in *A Starchamber Inquiry: A James Joyce Centennial Volume, 1882–1982,* ed. E. L. Epstein (New York: Methuen Publishing, 1982), 155–64, and, more recently, Michael H. Begnal, *Dreamscheme: Narrative and Voice in "Finnegans Wake"* (Syra-

cuse, N.Y.: Syracuse University Press, 1988; hereafter cited in text)—as opposed to Margot Norris, *The Decentered Universe of "Finnegans Wake"* (Baltimore: Johns Hopkins University Press, 1976), and Bishop.

16. Patrick McCarthy, "The Structures and Meanings of *Finnegans Wake,*" in *A Companion to Joyce Studies,* 605.

Chapter Six

1. Richard Ellmann, *Ulysses on the Liffey* (New York: Oxford University Press, 1972), p. 17.

2. See Ellmann's summary of Aristotle's influence on Joyce in *Ulysses on the Liffey,* 12–17. See also Peterson, Cohn, and Epstein, 25–27, and Umberto Eco, *The Aesthetics of Chaosmos: The Middle Ages of James Joyce* (Tulsa, Okla.: University of Tulsa Press, 1982).

3. Mary Reynolds, *Joyce and Dante: The Shaping Imagination* (Princeton, N.J.: Princeton University Press, 1981), 11.

4. William York Tindall, *James Joyce: His Way of Interpreting the Modern World* (New York: Scribner's, 1950), 2–3.

5. For a discussion of Joyce and modernism, see, for example, Heyward Ehrlich, ed., *Light Rays: James Joyce and Modernism* (New York: New Horizon Press, 1983), and W. J. McCormack and Alistair Stead, eds., *James Joyce and Modern Literature* (London: Routledge, 1982).

6. Valerie Eliot, ed., *The Waste Land: A Facsimile and Transcript of the Original Drafts Including the Annotations of Ezra Pound* (New York: Harcourt Brace, 1971), 9, 12.

7. Robert Martin Adams, *AfterJoyce* (New York: Oxford University Press, 1977), 3.

8. See Vivian Mercier, *The New Novel from Queneau to Pinget* (New York: Farrar, Straus, and Giroux, 1971), and Breon Mitchell, *James Joyce and the German Novel, 1922–1933* (Athens: Ohio University Press, 1976). For Joyce and American writers, see Craig Hansen Werner's *Paradoxical Resolutions: American Fiction since James Joyce* (Urbana: Univ. of Illinois, 1982).

9. For a summary of views on Joyce's temporal world, see Margaret Church, "Time as an Organizing Principle in the Fiction of James Joyce," in *Work in Progress,* 70–81. For varied discussions of Freud and Marx, see, for example, the essays on Freud in Bernard Benstock, ed., *The Seventh of Joyce* (Bloomington: Indiana University Press, 1982), 51–85, and those on Marx in Bernard Benstock, ed., *James Joyce: The Augmented Ninth,* (Syracuse, N.Y.: Syracuse University Press, 1988), 309–45. For a collection of essays on Joyce and psychoanalytic theory, see *James Joyce Quarterly* 13, no. 3 (1976): 266–384. See also Sheldon Brivic, *Joyce between Freud and Jung* (Port Washington: Kennikat Press, 1980), and Mark Shechner, *Joyce in Nighttown: A Psychoanalytic Inquiry into "Ulysses"* (Berkeley: University of California Press, 1974).

10. See Cheryl Herr, *Joyce's Anatomy of Culture* (Urbana: University of Illinois Press, 1986); see also R. B. Kershner, *Joyce, Bahktin, and Popular Literature: Chronicles of Disorder* (Chapel Hill: University of North Carolina Press, 1989).

11. For a discussion of the Irishness of Joyce within the context of English and Continental literature, see Bernard Benstock, *James Joyce: The Undiscovered Country* (Dublin: Gill, 1977). For a discussion of Joyce within a political context, see Dominic Manganiello, *Joyce's Politics* (London: Routledge, 1980). For recent studies of Joyce and authority, see Restuccia, and see Vicki Mahaffey, *Reauthorizing Joyce* (Cambridge, England: Cambridge University Press, 1988). For recent feminist readings, see Bonnie Kime Scott, *James Joyce* (Atlantic Highlands, N.J.: Humanities Press, 1987), and the essays in Bonnie Kime Scott, ed., *New Alliances in Joyce Studies* (Newark: University of Delaware Press, 1988), 113–192.

12. See, for example, Colin MacCabe, *James Joyce and the Revolution of the Word* (London: Macmillan, 1978); Colin MacCabe, ed., *James Joyce: New Perspectives* (Sussex: Harvester, 1982); Derek Attridge and Daniel Ferrer, eds., *Post-structuralist Joyce: Essays from the French* (Cambridge, England: Cambridge University Press, 1984); and the introduction and discussions of theory, including the opening essay by Jacques Derrida, in *The Augmented Ninth*. For an excellent summary of the historical patterns in Joyce studies, see Bernard Benstock, "Assimilating James Joyce," in *Critical Essays on James Joyce*, ed. Bernard Benstock (Boston: G. K. Hall, 1985); hereafter cited in text.

Selected Bibliography

PRIMARY SOURCES

Fiction

Dubliners. New York: Viking Press, 1967
Finnegans Wake. New York: Viking Press, 1939.
A Portrait of the Artist as a Young Man. New York: Viking Press, 1964.
Ulysses. New York: Random House, 1961. Also *Ulysses: The Corrected Text*.
    New York: Random House, 1986.

Poetry

Collected Poems. New York: Viking Press, 1957.

Drama

Exiles. New York: Penguin, 1973.

Miscellaneous

The Critical Writings of James Joyce. Edited by Ellsworth Mason and Richard
    Ellmann. New York: Viking Press, 1959.
Giacomo Joyce. Edited by Richard Ellmann. New York: Viking Press, 1968.
Letters of James Joyce. Vol. 1, edited by Stuart Gilbert; vols. 2 and 3, edited by
    Richard Ellmann. New York: Viking Press, 1966.
Selected Letters of James Joyce. Edited by Richard Ellmann. New York: Viking
    Press, 1975.
Stephen Hero. Edited by John J. Slocum and Herbert Cahoon. New York: New
    Directions, 1963.

SECONDARY SOURCES

The bibliography of secondary sources is limited to the works most often
    helpful to the beginning student of Joyce. Many of the specialized studies
    of Joyce have already been cited in the text and notes.
Adams, Robert M. *After Joyce: Studies in Fiction after "Ulysses."* New York:
    Oxford University Press, 1977. Adams's book evaluates Joyce's direct and

sometimes indirect influence on 14 modern writers, including Woolf, Faulkner, Beckett, O'Brien, Nabokov, and Borges.

Benstock, Bernard, ed. *James Joyce: The Augmented Ninth.* Proceedings of the Ninth International James Joyce Symposium, Frankfurt, 1984. Syracuse, N.Y.: Syracuse University Press, 1988. This collection of essays stands out among the several volumes from other Joyce symposia because of its claims for historical significance in Joyce scholarship in its recording of the shift in Joyce's studies to a greater awareness and acceptance of deconstruction and poststructuralism.

Bowen, Zack, and James Carens, eds. *A Companion to Joyce Studies.* Westport, Conn.: Greenwood Press, 1984. This massive collection of essays attempts coverage of the entire body of Joyce's work. The essays, written by authoritative Joyce scholars, are directed at "serious readers who need assistance after having read Joyce's works for the first time" (xii).

Budgen, Frank. *James Joyce and the Making of "Ulysses."* London: Grayson, 1934 (reissued with additional materials in 1972 by Oxford University Press). Budgen's book is regarded by Clive Hart and Hugh Kenner as the best ever written on Joyce. As an aid to *Ulysses* it follows Gilbert's *James Joyce's "Ulysses"* (1930) and precedes valuable works by Kain, Ellmann, Goldberg, Hayman, French, Lawrence, Kenner, and others cited in the text.

Deming, Robert H., ed. *A Bibliography of James Joyce Studies.* 2d ed. Boston: G. K. Hall, 1977. Deming's secondary bibliography covers Joyce studies to 1973. The student should also consult the "Current JJ Checklist," prepared by Alan M. Cohn until his death in 1989, in *James Joyce Quarterly* and the "Annual James Joyce Checklist" in *Joyce Studies Annual.*

Dunleavy, Janet Egleson, ed. *Classics of Joyce Criticism.* Urbana: University of Illinois Press, 1990. These essays, written by the Benstocks, Bowen, Hart, Senn, Staley, and others, present an overview of the "classic works" of Joyce criticism by such scholars as Ellmann, Kain, Kenner, Levin, and Tindall and the influence of their introductory, comparative, and resource studies on subsequent generations of Joyce readers and critics.

Ellmann, Richard. *James Joyce.* Rev. ed. New York: Oxford University Press, 1982. This standard biography of Joyce is also an exceptional work of scholarship and criticism. Ellmann's biography is a monumental work in Joyce studies.

————. *The Consciousness of Joyce.* New York: Oxford University Press, 1977. Ellmann's attempt to measure Joyce's consciousness and conscious use of principal sources includes such obvious literary works as the *Odyssey* and *Hamlet.* The book draws on Joyce's Trieste library and includes an embellished appendix of Joyce's library in 1920. See also Michael Patrick Gillespie, *James Joyce's Trieste Library* (Austin: University of Texas Press, 1986).

Gifford, Don, and Robert J. Seidman. *Notes for Joyce: "Dubliners" and "A Portrait of the Artist as a Young Man."* New York: E. P. Dutton, 1967. *Joyce Annotated: Notes for "Dubliners" and "A Portrait of the Artist as a Young Man."* Berkeley: University of California Press, 1982. *Notes for Joyce: An Annotation of Joyce's "Ulysses."* New York: E. P. Dutton, 1974. *"Ulysses" Annotated.* Berkeley: University of California Press, 1989. These handbooks are useful guides to the reading of *Dubliners, A Portrait,* and *Ulysses.* Readers of *Ulysses* should also consult Weldon Thornton, *Allusions in "Ulysses": An Annotated List* (Chapel Hill: University of North Carolina Press, 1968).

Gilbert, Stuart. *James Joyce's "Ulysses": A Study.* London: Faber and Faber, 1930. 2d ed., rev. and enlarged. New York: Random House, Vintage Books, 1955. Gilbert's influential study of *Ulysses* was encouraged, assisted, and endorsed by Joyce. It offers a detailed, chapter-by-chapter commentary on the Homeric correspondences and a discussion of the "leading themes" of *Ulysses.*

Hart, Clive. *Structure and Motif in "Finnegans Wake."* Evanston, Ill.: Northwestern University Press, 1962. Hart's book is regarded as a pivotal work in *Wake* scholarship. As an aid to *Finnegans Wake,* it follows the *Skeleton Key* of Campbell and Robinson, Glasheen's first *Census,* and Atherton's *Books at the Wake* and precedes valuable works by Benstock, Norris, McHugh, Bishop, and others cited in the text.

Kain, Richard M. *Dublin in the Age of William Butler Yeats.* Norman: University of Oklahoma Press, 1962. Kain's book is an early but valuable background study of Joyce, especially his relationship with the writers of the Irish Renaissance.

Kenner, Hugh. *Dublin's Joyce.* Bloomington: Indiana University Press, 1956. Kenner's book has provided a focus for several important discussions in Joyce studies, especially because of its controversial view of Stephen Dedalus. The author of several important books on Joyce, Kenner has become a major presence in Joyce criticism.

Kershner, R. B. *Joyce, Bakhtin, and Popular Literature: Chronicles of Disorder.* Chapel Hill: University of North Carolina Press, 1989. Awarded the American Conference for Irish Studies Prize for Literary Criticism, Kershner's book is a thorough examination of the influence of popular literature on *Dubliners, A Portrait,* and *Exiles.*

Levin, Harry. *James Joyce: A Critical Introduction.* Norfolk, Conn.: New Directions, 1941; rev. and augmented ed. 1960. Levin's introduction is generally regarded as a pioneering work in establishing Joyce's readership and critical reputation. More recent introductions include books by Benstock, Parrinder, and Scott.

Manganiello, Dominic. *Joyce's Politics.* London: Routledge and Kegan Paul, 1980. While many critics have assumed Joyce was indifferent to politics,

Manganiello effectively demonstrates Joyce's constant awareness not only of Irish politics but of the modern political ideas and affairs of Europe.

Peake, C. H. *James Joyce: The Citizen and the Artist*. Stanford: Stanford University Press, 1977. Peake's book is a sound, thorough study of *Dubliners, A Portrait*, and *Ulysses*, as well as a good starting place for the student of Joyce. Also recommended are the criticism and notes in the Viking Critical Library editions of *Dubliners* (ed. A. Walton Litz [New York: Viking Press, 1969]) and *A Portrait* (ed. Chester G. Anderson [New York: Viking Press, 1968]) for important introductory and background material.

Slocum, John J., and Herbert Cahoon, eds. *A Bibliography of James Joyce (1882–1941)*. New Haven, Conn.: Yale University Press, 1953; rep., Westport, Conn.: Greenwood Press, 1971. This primary bibliography, covering Joyce's published work up to 1950 with occasional subsequent additions, remains the standard work.

Staley, Thomas F. "James Joyce." In *Anglo-Irish Literature: A Review of Research*, edited by Richard J. Finneran. New York: Modern Language Association of America, 1976. "James Joyce." In *Recent Research on Anglo-Irish Writers*, edited by Richard J. Finneran. New York: Modern Language Association, 1983. Staley's review and later supplement of Joyce research are reliable and informative narrative guides. Other guides are Staley's *An Annotated Critical Bibliography of James Joyce* (New York: Harvester Wheatsheaf, 1989) and Thomas Rice's earlier *James Joyce: A Guide to Research* (New York: Garland, 1982).

Tindall, William York. *James Joyce: His Way of Interpreting the Modern World*. New York: Scribner's, 1950. Tindall is widely known for his reader's guides to Joyce's works, including *Finnegans Wake*. Tindall's *James Joyce* is an important early work on Joyce's relationship to modern art and his use of symbol and myth.

Index

The Author

Richard F. Peterson is a professor and currently chair of the Department of English at Southern Illinois University at Carbondale. He is the author of *Mary Lavin* (1978) and *William Butler Yeats* (1982) in Twayne's English Authors Series. He has also coedited, with Alan Cohn and Edmund Epstein, *Work in Progress: Joyce Centenary Essays*. His essays on Joyce and other Irish writers have appeared in various journals, annuals, and collections devoted to modern and Anglo-Irish literature.

Professor Peterson has taught at Southern Illinois since 1969. He has been honored on several occasions by his department, college, and university for his teaching excellence at the undergraduate and graduate levels.